Elihu Root
and the
Conservative Tradition

The Library of American Biography

EDITED BY OSCAR HANDLIN

Richard W. Leopold

Elihu Root
and the
Conservative
Tradition

Edited by Oscar Handlin

Little, Brown and Company · *Boston*

C

Published simultaneously in Canada
by Little, Brown & Company (Canada) Limited

PRINTED IN THE UNITED STATES OF AMERICA

To
Gray Cowan Boyce

Editor's Preface

THE LOT of the conservative in America has not been an easy one. In a society given to radical rapid change, he has been the advocate of caution. Against those who argued the advantages of the continually new, he has preached the utility of the old. In a society without firmly fixed institutions, and without the stabilizing influences of traditionally established systems of law and religion, the conservative labored always under a handicap.

The European patterns of conservatism therefore never became acclimatized in the United States; and those who wished to slacken the pace of change worked out for themselves a philosophy that acknowledged the inevitability of change, but within stable, restraining forms.

To maintain such a position intellectually was itself an imposing task. What was more, American conservatism was not, as it had been in Europe, rooted in a stable class structure. In the United States there existed neither a nobility nor a landed gentry to supply the leadership, nor a peasantry for the mass following. Indeed, the rural population, debt-laden and suffering in disadvantageous market situations, was often in the forefront of radical movements.

In the definition of American conservatism, therefore, the lead generally fell into the hands of lawyers, who were most sensitive to the restraints of the legal system and who wished to extend those restraints to all politics. Among those who defined American conservatism, none was more important than Elihu Root. Root appeared at that critical juncture in American history when the evolving industrial economy of the nation produced men of wealth who needed the support of a conservative tradition; and he was among the lawyers who, for reasons of their own, supplied that need. COVERING

This study examines the development of Root's career and locates it in the evolution of a conservative tradition in America. It thus raises the more general questions of how that tradition appeared, and of what function it served in the foreign affairs and domestic life of a nation that was primarily committed to rapid change. In doing so it throws valuable light upon a significant phase of our past.

OSCAR HANDLIN

Contents

Elihu Root

and the

Conservative Tradition

I

Acquisitive America:

The Making of a Conservative   1845-1899

IN THE SUMMER of 1899, President William McKinley was seeking a new Secretary of War. With his first term more than half completed, he was disturbed by an increasing criticism of his administration that not even unparalleled prosperity at home and the record of a successful war abroad could quell. The undertone of uneasiness and uncertainty that pervaded the nation as the century drew to a close stemmed directly from several baffling and unprecedented problems bequeathed by the smashing victory over Spain a year before. A prompt and honorable solution of them was imperative if the conscience of the American people was to be satisfied, and the head of the War Department would necessarily be the key figure in the process of adjustment.

For a variety of reasons — emotional, strategic, and economic — the United States had taken up arms in April 1898 to free Cuba and had emerged from the brief struggle with Spain with a colonial empire stretching from the South China Sea to the Caribbean. The annexation of Hawaii in July 1898 had been reasonably well debated and thought out in advance, but the acquisition of Puerto Rico, Guam, and the Philippines by the treaty of December 1898 had not been foreseen nor had the consequences thereof been fully appreciated. Many contemporaries and some historians, confusing cause and effect, have accused the McKinley administration, or a small expansionist group within the Republican party, of planned aggression; but a sounder explanation is that the President and his advisers were carried along by the logic of events, by a vague sense of duty and destiny, and by the belated realization that it was simpler to hold on to the Spanish conquests than to give them up.

Yet in planting the Stars and Stripes in distant, tropical climes, over peoples of different races, languages, and political traditions, the United States raised vital ethical, constitutional, and diplomatic questions to be hotly debated by its citizens for several years. Could a republic possess dependencies and retain its democratic character? Did the immortal Declaration of 1776 prohibit government without the consent of the governed? Did the Constitution and its guarantees of personal liberties follow the flag? What administrative machinery would be required to care for the islands? Were colonies economically profitable? Would foreign adventures retard the progress of reform at home? Would imperialism lead to wars and to the destruction of a long-cherished isolationism?

Already by July 1899, the answers to some of these questions were in the making. The Senate had approved the treaty of peace, with its territorial additions, by the narrowest of margins; but Americans were badly divided as to whether that vote meant a temporary occupation of the islands, a longer period of preparation for eventual independence, or the establishment of a permanent colonial status. To complicate a confused situation, a rebellion had erupted in the Philippines in February 1899. Five months later the conflagration was still raging, unchecked, with all the fury, cruelty, and desperation of a war for freedom against remote rulers of a different race. Uncertain of their purpose, uncomfortable in their role of conquerors, rather than of liberators, the American people were experiencing a sense of frustration from a conflict they did not want and which their leaders seemed powerless to end.

The War Department assumed, at this juncture, an importance unsurpassed in previous times of peace. Its immediate task was to put down the bloody and unpopular Filipino Insurrection. Its larger mission was to control and supervise the overseas possessions. Its incumbent, Russell A. Alger, had already proved himself incapable of coping with the demands placed upon his office by America's emergence as a world power. His record during the war with Spain had been constantly under fire. Accusations of inefficiency, most of them well grounded, and a series of scandals, large and small, had so dismayed the President that he had appointed a special commission to investigate the matter. Its report, submitted in February 1899, was, in effect, a scathing condemnation of past mistakes and a stern warning that the army must be reorganized, both in Washington and in the field, if it was to discharge successfully its new responsibilities.

When Alger reluctantly resigned on July 19, 1899, McKinley chose as his successor a first-class lawyer, not a military expert. For the President, the formulation of a colonial policy and the administration of an insular empire took precedence over reorganization of the armed forces. For that reason, he turned, not to a man who had worn the uniform, such as Theodore Roosevelt, who would have gladly exchanged his gubernatorial chair in Albany for a seat in the cabinet, but to a recognized leader of the New York bar, Elihu Root.

At fifty-four, Root was virtually unknown on the national political scene. Although long active in municipal and state affairs, he had held but two public offices. He had been United States Attorney for the District of Southern New York from 1883–1885, and he had served in the New York Constitutional Convention of 1894. His primary concern had been the law; and in that profession he had attained great prestige, especially as counsel to the powerful corporations that dominated American economic life after the Civil War.

In many ways, Root was the perfect solution to McKinley's search. He had an extraordinary talent for finding workable solutions to technical and complex problems. His integrity was unchallenged, his capacity for sustained labor unlimited, his deftness in placating suspicious legislators unexcelled, and his Republican orthodoxy unimpeachable. He was a delightful companion, a loyal friend, and a man without ambition for personal political advancement.

Thanks to his selection by McKinley, Root rapidly emerged as one of the most significant figures in recent American history. As Secretary of War from 1899–1904, he established a sound colonial system, modernized the army's high command, and created the General Staff Corps. As Secretary of State from 1905–1909, he strove to adjust diplomacy to the country's new place in world affairs, sought to promote peace by machinery that accorded with national traditions, and injected a spirit of good neighborliness into dealings with the states of the Western Hemisphere. As Senator from New York from 1909–1915, overborne by the onrush of a progressivism he could not accept, he waged a sincere, sane, rear-guard defense of conservatism. During the First World War, he championed the Allied cause, criticized Wilsonian neutrality, and belatedly advocated American intervention. During the subsequent peacemaking, he charted the original course of the reservationists and offered to Wilson a practical alternative, that was neither unfriendly nor destructive, to the controversial Covenant of the League of Nations. As an elder statesman after 1921, he attempted to assuage the animosities engendered by the battle over the Treaty of Versailles, and he stood forth as the most prominent proponent of America's entry into the World Court.

People at the time and historians since have wondered whether Root would not have been a wiser choice for the Republican Presidential nomination in 1908 than Taft, or in 1916 than Hughes. It has been argued that his sound judgment and rare appreciation of what was politically possible would have prevented a party split after 1910 and prepared the nation more adequately for warmaking and peacemaking after 1917. Actually, Root could never have been a successful popular leader. He was handicapped by his temperament and disqualified by his earlier legal activity.

This basic weakness was clearly grasped in 1915, when he voluntarily retired from the United States Senate, by the *New Republic,* probably the most intelligent organ of liberal thought of the day. That weekly paid high tribute to his ability, usefulness, and "disinterested devotion to the public good." It noted, however, that few Americans shed any tears over his withdrawal. The answer to this apparent paradox it found partly in the popular distrust of Root because he had once been a corporation attorney, but mainly in his own failure to grasp the larger moral issues of the hour. "The inability to do formative thinking," the editor concluded, "may not greatly handicap a statesman, but the moral and intellectual timidity which often accompanies the limitation is a fatal drawback. Elihu Root has failed to fire the imagination of his fellow citizens, not merely because he has lacked initiative but because he has lacked vision. . . . No man can lead a people who has his back to the future."

This perceptive but ex parte judgment, rendered at the flood tide of progressivism, points up not only the timeless conflict between liberalism and conservatism, but also the dilemma of the exemplar of the conservative tradition in twentieth-century American politics. As Thomas Jefferson once wrote, "Men, according to their constitutions, and the circumstances in which they are placed, differ honestly in opinion." Because of his constitution and the circumstances in which he was placed — or, to state it another way, because of his family background, legal career, mental processes, and position in society — Elihu Root was proud to bear the title of conservative. Since conservatism is a major key to his life and thought, it is well to recall some of the fundamental attributes of that philosophy and then, because the concept is not a static one, to indicate the kind of conservative Root was.

A conservative is one who keeps or guards. In contrast to a liberal, who seeks to extend freedom, he is disposed to maintain, preserve, uphold, and defend the established order. It does not follow, of course, that a conservative is opposed to all change; but he is cautious about innovation and the abandonment of the tested and tried. Where the liberal is sanguine and even optimistic about the future, the conservative is skeptical and sometimes pessimistic. He reveres the past and attempts to carry on its proved principles. So far as government is concerned, both philosophies claim to promote the welfare of the individual, but the conservative usually distrusts man in the mass and prefers to be ruled by the educated and propertied groups. A liberal is more interested in ends than in means, in the aims of government rather than in its administration. It is the general, not the specific, that attracts his attention.

Because he was intelligent and realistic, and because his adult life extended from the days of Ulysses S. Grant to those of Franklin D. Roosevelt, Root's conservatism is not easily categorized. He was no blind reactionary; and at times, especially in the last years of Theodore Roosevelt's

Presidency, he tolerated policies that were distinctly liberal for their day. But he always insisted that change be orderly and slow, that it respect existing institutions and interests, and that it recognize the American creed of a government of laws, not of men. Like most conservatives, he emphasized efficient administration, balanced power with responsibility, venerated the judicial process, and sought stability in all aspects of human relations. Order was his passion, whether he was concerned with the sugar refining industry, the management of colonies, military command relationships, or the codification of international law.

As he gained a closer knowledge of public affairs, Root modified some views he had held as a corporation counsel. But many beliefs remained fixed. He consistently opposed government encroachment upon the life of the individual, whether it affected property rights or personal liberties. He was confident that the enlightened self-interest of the business community would bring the greatest happiness to the greatest numbers. He had a deep respect for law and for legal procedures. He fought almost every alteration of the Constitution and was convinced that judicial review, even as practiced between 1890 and 1910, was the most valuable contribution his people had made to political science. He shared many of the ideas of Herbert Spencer and William Graham Sumner but voiced them less bluntly. He would have been pleased to be regarded as a latter-day Alexander Hamilton, though he possessed a less fertile mind and a less daring temperament than his fellow New Yorker. And yet, when all his strengths and weaknesses are added up, Elihu Root stands out as the ablest, most constructive conservative in American public life since 1900.

1. *Inheritance and Early Career*

The conservatism of Elihu Root is easily explained. Everything in his family heritage, his youthful environment, and his early professional career stimulated pride in American institutions and led him to feel that his was the land of opportunity and, even more important, of fulfillment. Life was good to Root; and while he may have denied that this was the best of all possible worlds, he did believe that application, initiative, brains, thrift, and integrity received their just reward. Realistic and unsentimental about most things, he discerned no essential flaw in the acquisitive America of the post-Civil War period; and he agreed with, though he would never himself have put them in cold print, the eulogistic views of Andrew Carnegie's *Triumphant Democracy*.

Root's forebears figured prominently in colonial and revolutionary annals. John Roote landed on American shores in 1639; a great-grandfather gave the order to open fire at Concord Bridge; and several ancestors fought against Burgoyne. This background gave Root a personal identification with his country's growth such as could not have been shared in the 1890's by Italian laborers in New York slums or by Scandinavian farmers on the Great Plains.

Root also reflected his early environment. Born on February 15, 1845, in the village of Clinton in central New York, the son of a professor of mathematics at Hamilton College, he long manifested the influence of a cultured but unpretentious upbringing amid the pastoral calm of a self-sufficient community. Educated in local academies and tutored by his father, he entered Hamilton in the momentous autumn of 1860 and graduated with high distinction four years later. Nothing in this environment prepared Root for the perplexing, ethical questions that an ascendant business group raised in the new, industrial America. Nothing gave him a firsthand acquaintance with adversity, with poverty, with social unrest, or with labor agitation, municipal corruption, and racial discrimination.

The contribution of the parents to the making of a conservative is less easily demonstrated. Root's mother, who seems to have been overshadowed by her spouse, was gentle, sensitive, and deeply religious. Hers was a restraining hand. Professor Oren Root, "Cube" Root as he was known to generations of Hamilton men, on the other hand, provided a persuasive example of an intellectual who was not aloof from the world of reality and of a scientist who could bring the practicality of his discipline into the home. Yet Oren Root was no social reformer, no crusader, convinced the times were out of joint. Even on a meager professorial salary, the father found life rewarding and the *status quo* pleasant.

The years in which young Root grew to manhood likewise nurtured conservative inclinations. The Civil War, to be sure, failed to affect him, as it failed to divert many of his college generation. Enrollments declined, but there was no wholesale disruption of academic life as in 1917 or 1941. In common with such diverse personages as John D. Rockefeller, Henry Adams, Henry George, and William Dean Howells, Root sat out the war. An enlistment as a private in the New York militia in October 1864 constituted his military contribution.

It was less the stirring events of 1861–1865 than the far-reaching changes of 1865–1900 that shaped the thought and outlook of Elihu Root. The postwar years were ones of boom and industrial growth, punctuated, to be sure, by occasional depressions and by a more prolonged and per-

sistent agricultural impoverishment; but for the ambitious
and the bold there were golden opportunities in transportation, manufacturing, and finance, as well as in the law
which counseled the corporations in those fields. It was
to law that Root turned in 1865, and it was to the thriving
metropolis on Manhattan Island that he set his course.
He was the first of his clan, as he put it, "to take the back
trail," the trail of advancement that had heretofore led
westward, but which now pointed, as if to mark the end
of an era, away from the setting sun. Such a career in such
a setting confirmed and entrenched his conservative pro-
clivities.

After 1865, Root climbed rapidly up the ladder of the
New York bar and enjoyed a steady, though less spectacular ascent on the rungs of society, wealth, and local politics. He entered New York University Law School in the
fall of 1865, and despite time off to support himself through
teaching in fashionable female institutions, he received
his degree and was admitted to practice in the middle
of 1867. A decade of intensive labor ensued, long hours that
taxed mind and body, all inspired by a determination to
be "a lawyer first and all the time."

A strict — some believe an overly strict — interpretation
of a lawyer's duties cast a momentary shadow in 1871–
1873 over Root's promising career. He served at that time
as a junior counsel in the criminal trial of the notorious
William M. Tweed, accused of bribery and gross fraud in
New York city contracts. Although his association with the
case did not affect the outcome in any way, it did brand
Root for all time as the defender of a corrupt boss and
persuaded many persons that he would accept anyone as
a client. Politically, it was an incident he could never live
down.

The usual explanation for his action is that Root was
adhering to the code which obliged a lawyer to assist even

the most heinous villain until a verdict of guilt is returned. To some, such a justification has seemed strained. It is one thing, they have argued, for a famous trial advocate like Clarence Darrow to feel in 1924 that he must, when appealed to, try to prevent the execution of two youthful killers; but Root was under no such moral compulsion. Tweed's freedom and even his life did not depend upon an additional young attorney. The presiding judge felt that Root could have refused the retainer without incurring the slightest criticism, for he pointedly declared that "good faith to a client never can justify or require bad faith to your own consciences." Others, however, have seen in Root's course evidence of great moral courage, such as might be shown today by a young liberal lawyer agreeing to defend a known Communist.

However much the Tweed episode hurt Root in later public life, it did not check his professional advancement after 1873. His practice grew by leaps and bounds and involved contests over estates, railroad suits, bank problems, and cases affecting municipal affairs in New York. He traveled frequently and widely, gained renown as an effective trial advocate, and in 1881 was permitted to argue before the Supreme Court of the United States. Not until after 1885 did Root become a corporation attorney in the sense that his primary concern was devising means by which big-business groups could organize, consolidate, and operate without fear of litigation or state interference.

The reasons for Root's success as a lawyer were many. He was a hard worker, with vast powers of concentration and endurance, who spared neither himself, his family, nor his colleagues. A retentive memory and an ability to master detail made him devastating in the courtroom and almost invincible in cross-examination. In some areas he was widely read and could be called learned; but it was his wisdom, calmness, and lack of pretense that drew people to him for counsel and advice. He could strip complex issues to their essentials and suggest procedures that were as simple as they were effectual.

One other asset eased Root's path in the law, just as it later did in public office. That was an irrepressible sense of humor that kept his associates constantly amused and lifted prosaic matters into the realm of mirth. For example, in 1908, when a directive prohibiting Sunday work by government employees reached the State Department, Root acknowledged it as follows: "I shall see hereafter that such work is confined strictly to the Secretary and Assistant Secretaries. Would it be deemed improper if we were to do work on Sunday regarding the affairs of the Far East where it is already Monday, and transfer our labors as Monday comes around and Sunday recedes, westward through the Near East and Europe?"

Root's legal triumphs were paralleled by social and material progress. Many of his clients were leaders of New York society and finance; with some of them he established lasting friendships. In 1869 he joined the Union League Club, a stronghold of Republicanism and of the well-to-do. That institution played an important part in his daily life; but, of more immediate significance, it brought him into contact with Salem H. Wales, a generous and genteel philanthropist. In 1877, Root was introduced to Wales's charming daughter, Clara Frances. After a brief courtship in the Adirondacks, the young couple announced their engagement in October. Three months later they were married. The parents-in-law provided Root with a luxurious town house at 30 East Fifty-fifth Street, an address that was exchanged in 1886 for 25 East Sixty-ninth. Summers were spent, until the end of the century, at Southampton, Long Island, and thereafter at Clinton. Three children added to Root's happiness, Edith in 1878, Elihu, Jr. in 1881, and Edward Wales in 1884. From all accounts, Root was an affectionate father and a devoted husband, who drew strength and inspiration from his family.

2. The Problem of the "Corporation Lawyer"

The central problem of Root's career before 1899 was his role as counsel for various powerful business interests in and around New York. This work, indisputably successful from the point of view of his clients, earned him the politically fatal title of "corporation lawyer." In a different climate of opinion, the popular estimate of that work blocked any possibility of his nomination for the Presidency.

In appraising Root's services for large corporate groups, it should be remembered that the code of business ethics was markedly lower in the late nineteenth century than it is today. Although the historian cannot ignore the manifold evils that stemmed from the law of the jungle in industry and from the appalling economic inequalities in society, he has an obligation to describe the business leaders and their counselors in the light of criteria that then prevailed. As Root told the biographer of Chester A. Arthur in 1927, "It is imperative to assess and explain actions by the standards and ideas of the time in which they occur."

Two examples of Root's corporate practice will suffice. One was his association with the Havemeyer refining companies, the infamous Sugar Trust. In 1880, when Root was first retained by the Havemeyers, there was, as yet, no monopoly. Root's earliest activity consisted of conducting suits to recover payments for excessive duties and of suggesting how to avoid needless litigation. Not until October 1887 was an agreement perfected whereby seventeen companies, possessing among them about 78 per cent of the refining capacity of the nation, placed their destinies in the hands of eleven trustees. What part, if any, Root played in this move for a more unified control we do not know.

In 1890 popular agitation against industrial monopoly culminated in passage by Congress of the Sherman Anti-Trust Act. That same year the initial device adopted in 1887 to destroy competition among the refiners of sugar cane, the trustee plan — copied from Standard Oil — was declared illegal by the New York Circuit Court of Appeals. That tribunal held the delegation of powers involved in the trusteeship scheme to be a perversion of the company's charter, and it ordered the dissolution of the North River Sugar Refining Company. The Havemeyers then turned to Root to find some other legal method for controlling subsidiary units.

Taking advantage of a recent change in the corporation statutes of New Jersey, Root recommended the formation in that state of a property holding company. The subsequent reorganization was highly satisfactory to his clients; within a few years the new American Sugar Refining Company controlled substantially 98 per cent of the national output.

There is no evidence that Root's legal acumen was used by the Havemeyers to defeat a later suit to break up the Sugar Trust for violation of the Sherman Act. The Supreme Court's verdict in the famous Knight case in January 1895, in which it drew a distinction between monopoly in manufacture and monopoly in interstate commerce, was the result, not of skillful arguing by company lawyers, but of a blundering presentation of the facts by the government. In 1910, Root told Taft that he had always felt that the court's decision had been based upon a too narrow consideration of the facts, but there is no contemporary record of his displeasure over the ruling, or of his belief that a mistake had been made.

Much better known than Root's connection with the Sugar Trust was his link with the Whitney-Ryan traction syndicate in New York. Thanks to muckrakers like Charles E. Russell, to partisan but reformist newspapers like the New York *World*, and, after 1906, to the politically hostile and personally embittered William Randolph Hearst, Root's role in the consolidation of Manhattan's street railways, and the accompanying financial abuses, received a very full, if not always accurate, airing.

The key figures in this consolidation were William C. Whitney and Thomas F. Ryan. Whitney was the scion of an old New England family, lieutenant of Samuel J. Tilden in his battle against the Tweed Ring, father of the revitalized American navy, and leader of the conservative Eastern wing of the Democratic party. Ryan, also a Democrat, was a self-made Virginian of extraordinary talent and inordinate ambition. Root was long on intimate personal terms with both, and from them he caught the spirit of Wall Street and high finance.

Root's connection with the group began in 1886; and for the next thirteen years his resourceful brain and superb courtroom technique were invaluable in obtaining municipal franchises, blocking by injunction rival endeavors, alleviating tax burdens, and reorganizing mushrooming holdings into efficient and economical operating units. In general, Root told his clients what they could do, what the law permitted, and what it forbade. He had little concern with financial transactions, and he urged, where possible, a conservative and cautious policy in issuing new securities.

After 1899, while Root was gaining a national reputation for distinguished government administration, he and his old associates were subjected to a devastating and embarrassing attack by the muckrakers. Neither then nor later did Root disclose his innermost thoughts on his work for Whitney and Ryan, but they can be surmised. He felt strongly the obligation that a lawyer bore to his client; and while he would not prostitute himself to abet illegal action, he did believe he should help businessmen operate to the fullest advantage within the letter of the law. "It is not a function of law to enforce the rules of morality," he told Roosevelt in December 1899. "There is altogether too general an impression that it is immoral to acquire wealth, and far too little appreciation of the fact that the vast preponderance of the grand fortunes which now exist in this country have been amassed, not by injuring any living being, but as an incident to the conferring of great benefits on the community. . . . It is the protection of the individual against wrong to him that should be aimed at, and not any attempt to confine the acquisition of wealth by a statutory imposition."

Just how society in general rather than one individual in particular was to be protected from the predatory prac- tices of the captains of industry Root did not then say. To his credit, however, he later recognized his earlier uncon- cern, as an attorney, for the deeper significance of the law, in contrast to the rights of his clients. In 1906, when the muckrake tide was at its flood, he wrote privately, "The pure lawyer seldom concerns himself about the broad aspects of public policy . . . Lawyers are almost always conservative. Through insisting upon the maintenance of legal rules, they become instinctively opposed to change."

In short, there was nothing essentially discreditable in Root's work as a "corporation lawyer," nothing to justify the insinuations and accusations of the less temperate and less factual muckrakers and of the hostile political editors. Root followed the rules as he found them and played the game honestly. He did not often reflect upon the rules, and his concept of economic morality was better suited to rural Clinton than to metropolitan New York. His attitude was typical of the outstanding members of the bar, and it partook of the same virtues and the same defects. Integrity and intelligence were tempered by a failure to regard the law as a living organism and by a reluctance to look beyond its letter to its implications for society as a whole. With a conservative's obsession for order and stability, he was inclined to gloss over the unequal distribution of economic power and, thereby, of political influence. An unconcern for or an unawareness of the social injustices of the 1880's and 1890's, rather than a prostitution of his legal talents in behalf of corporate wealth, is the criticism that the historian in the middle of the twentieth century can level against Elihu Root.

3. *The Problem of a "Social Conscience"*

While Root was winning golden opinions before the New York bar and serving a multitude of rich clients, the fabric of American society was rapidly changing. The stupendous economic developments that unified transportation and communication, consolidated industry and business, expanded manufactures and agriculture, and facilitated the accumulation of gigantic personal fortunes left in their wake a host of alarming problems. The stratification of classes, the extremes of wealth and poverty, the unbalance of management and labor, the contrast between city and farm were issues that no thoughtful citizen could ignore. The agrarian revolt, the demand for currency reform, the attack upon the trusts, and the wave of bitter, bloody strikes all provided eloquent testimony that the American democratic faith was in peril at the very moment of magnificent material accomplishment. What, one may fairly ask, did Root think of these developments?

The question is more easily posed than answered. Root was always a man of few words, on paper or in speeches. Only occasionally can we document his failure to comprehend the social implications of the momentous transformation. In 1879, the year Henry George completed *Progress and Poverty,* Root delivered the commencement address at Hamilton. He was then thirty-four. After blaming the "better classes" for political apathy and after paying his respects to those corporations that "corrupt legislatures," he accused "the paupers and the laborers in the cities" and "the workmen in manufactories and mines" of the desire to destroy, not conserve, the nation's riches. He saw in the recent railroad strikes, in the demand for unlimited greenbacks, and in the Granger laws of the Western states "the war of poverty upon wealth."

Again in April 1881, during a long fight to remove three police commissioners for failing to keep New York streets clean, Root temporarily lowered his guard. Angered by the incessant popular criticism of his clients, he blurted out, half in exasperation and half in bravado, "We are not to be intimidated by the vulgar cry of an excited populace." In those few words, Root revealed his intellectual kinship with Alexander Hamilton and his inherent distrust of movements led by the people.

For the most part, however, Root remained silent on controversial nonpolitical issues. Hence we can only surmise his thoughts on the activity of labor unions, the use of injunctions to curb strikes, the battle with the slums, the amassing of huge private fortunes, and the long line of reactionary decisions by the Supreme Court. Not only as a lawyer but also as a citizen, Root seemed inured to the social evils of the day.

4. The Problem of "Political Loyalty"

The pattern of Root's political loyalty was a familiar one in acquisitive America of the post-Civil War era. To be a Republican first, last, and always was for many an article of faith and a symbol of respectability. It denoted fealty to the Union, an endorsement of the *status quo,* and an absence of social and economic heresies. A large number of Republicans were convinced that the Democrats were incapable of governing the country; a smaller, but still sizable group professed to believe that their rivals were bent upon destroying American ideals and institutions. These alarms found readier acceptance as social tension, fed by periodic depressions and unrequited injustices, increased near the century's close.

Root shared most of these preconceptions; but he was not, prior to 1899, prominent in high party circles. His activity was largely confined to the city and the state and, even there, not as a candidate for office. He did feel, however, that all citizens had a duty, not simply a right, to participate actively in politics; and he believed that the evils of the day were due less to the venality of the professionals than to the abstention of the "better elements" in society who regarded local government with scorn. Hence he gladly served on Republican county committees, presided over nominating conventions, and battled against the machine of both parties. He frequently advocated fusion as the best way to terminate the corrupt rule of Tammany Hall.

But political reform ended for Root, as it did for so many others with an equally commendable civic con-

science, with good government. He approached the complex problems of a sprawling metropolitan area in the
spirit of a voter in a New England town meeting. He made
no attempt to alter the existing economic and social structure that underlay municipal corruption. He gave no
thought to providing services for those groups that repaid
the bosses with support at the polls for small favors. He
revealed no appreciation of the intimate connection between new business enterprises, such as street railways,
and urban misrule.

There is no reason to believe that, before the war with
Spain, Root was much interested in foreign affairs. Five
days before the *Maine* blew up in Havana harbor, he insisted in an address at the Union League Club that "Bry-
anism" would be the paramount issue in the fall elections.
He did not share Roosevelt's eagerness for direct action
in Cuba or his desire for overseas expansion. By April 2,
1898, Root did feel that McKinley was delaying unduly,
and he warned a friend in the cabinet that "the President
should lead and not be pushed." War he then regarded as
inevitable. He was convinced that the Cuban cause was
just and that the American right to intervene was unimpeachable.

By 1899, Root had become acquainted with such later
associates as John Hay, William Howard Taft, Henry
Cabot Lodge, and Theodore Roosevelt. The tie with the
last was the oldest. The two men met, apparently, in 1881,
a year after Roosevelt was graduated from Harvard. That
autumn, Root helped eliminate an obstacle to Roosevelt's
nomination for the state legislature. Five years later,
after refusing to run himself, Root directed Roosevelt's
unsuccessful mayoralty campaign against Abram S. Hewitt
and Henry George. In 1898 it was Root again whose fertile
brain resolved the legal tangle that threatened to keep the
hero of San Juan Hill out of the governorship. Roosevelt

freely admitted that, without Root's aid, he would not have been declared eligible.

No similar debt of gratitude was owed to Root by William McKinley, either before or after he entered the White House. It is likely that Root contributed generously to the campaign fund in 1896, and he pleased the President-elect by persuading Cornelius N. Bliss to reconsider his initial refusal to take a cabinet post. For these reasons, perhaps, McKinley asked Root in the spring of 1897 to go to Madrid as minister to adjust the Cuban controversy. The New Yorker declined, not because he was the President's second or third choice, but because he felt that his inexperience in diplomacy and his ignorance of the Spanish language imposed insuperable handicaps.

More than two years were to elapse before McKinley again invited Root to enter the government service. This time he had a lawyer's job to be done, and Root accepted in a step that altered the course and tenor of his life. The conservative product of an acquisitive age gave up a lucrative practice and the comforts of private life to take the United States as his client and to become one of the outstanding Secretaries of War and Secretaries of State in American history.

I I

Imperialism:

Secretary of War 1899-1904

THE PROMPT ACCEPTANCE of McKinley's invitation of July 21, 1899, was a little surprising. Root's devotion to the bar was very real, his practice highly lucrative, and his wife extremely reluctant to leave New York. Moreover, he knew almost nothing about the army.

The President's assurance that he wanted Root for his legal talents, not his military knowledge, best explains the decision that transformed Root from a respected private citizen into an outstanding public official. Other forces were probably at work. Root always felt that in a democracy all citizens had a duty to participate in government. Perhaps he welcomed, at fifty-four, a different experience. Certainly he expected that his service would be relatively brief, not extending beyond McKinley's tenure. No one, least of all Root, would have predicted in 1899 that he would hold three important offices for almost sixteen consecutive years.

Root's success in the War Department was immediate and overwhelming. He brought to the task a keen, logical, incisive mind that went quickly to the heart of matters. His own tireless industry and devotion to duty inspired warm affection and the best efforts from his subordinates. He was, for the most part, an excellent administrator, who could master detail and delegate authority. To two Presidents of diametrically opposed temperaments and personalities he gave unswerving loyalty. Both McKinley and Roosevelt always regarded him as the strongest and most disinterested member of the cabinet.

Other reasons explain Root's success. His predecessor was an easy man to follow. Honest but inept, Alger had found the job too big for him. The inevitable demand for reform that led to his resignation smoothed the way for Root's plans and helped insure their adoption. McKinley's advisers, save for John Hay, were not outstanding figures; and even the latter was retiring, unaggressive, frequently ill, and utterly unable to deal with Congressmen. Roosevelt's cabinet was stronger, but Root was still the man who commanded most attention. He had, moreover, the ability few citizens possessed to understand the thinking of and to maintain the unqualified respect of the professional soldier.

In short, Root was presented with a splendid opportunity. The times were ripe for constructive thought and action. Without him, some changes would have come; but the magnitude and rapidity of the accomplishments and improvements in the War Department can be attributed largely to his intelligence, determination, and sense of timing.

1. Puerto Rico: The Colonial System Inaugurated

Although Root's most urgent tasks in July 1899 were to restore self-respect in the War Department and to insure sufficient manpower to suppress an insurrection in the Philippines, he faced simultaneously the perplexing and con-

troversial problem of defining a colonial policy for the
United States. With certain insular possessions he did not
have to deal. Hawaii, long the objective of expansionists,
was immediately granted a large measure of self-government and did not figure in the debate on imperialism.
Sparsely populated Guam, and later Tutuila, were entrusted to the navy, while uninhabited Wake, like Midway
before it, was virtually forgotten until the advent of
transpacific aerial navigation in the 1930's. Root's concern
was not with those colonies but with the Philippines,
Puerto Rico, and Cuba, the last of which was not formally
annexed but only temporarily occupied.

It was easiest for Root to begin with Puerto Rico. Unlike
the Philippines, the island was peaceful. Its proximity also
made first hand study simpler and foreign interference
less likely. In contrast to Cuba, there had been, prior to
1898, no devastating civil war and, after the American
landings, no real fighting. The demand for immediate
independence, strong in Cuba, was feeble in its neighbor.
And the relations of the United States with Puerto Rico
were not complicated by any pledge to grant freedom,
either at once or in the future. The main headaches Root
faced in Puerto Rico were economic.

Under Spanish rule, Puerto Rico had enjoyed free trade
with Cuba and the mother country. Annexation to the
United States meant the loss of those two tariff-free markets
without any compensation, for the high duties of the Dingley Act still applied to imports to the mainland. To make
matters worse, a tropical hurricane struck the island on
August 8, 1899, destroying two thirds of the coffee crop,
reducing 100,000 people to destitution, and disrupting
the already inadequate avenues of communication. Since
Puerto Rico was still under military rule, the responsibility
for relief was Root's. He promptly spent almost $400,000
out of contingent funds; and, as Congress was not in session

to vote extraordinary appropriations, he organized private charity to tide the islanders over the crisis.

Only exemption from the American tariff, however, would place Puerto Rico on a sound economic basis. But any breach in protectionism was, initially at least, distasteful to the businessman's administration of William McKinley. Root, like his superior, did not relish free trade; but when the welfare of his colonial wards clashed with the profits of American manufacturers and farmers, he was prepared to resolve the conflict in favor of the dependencies. Recognizing that there might be legal obstacles, Root advised the President on August 18 to exempt Puerto Rican products from the Dingley levies. In his state of the union message of December 5, 1899, McKinley accepted Root's counsel and told Congress that it was "our plain duty . . . to abolish all customs tariffs between the United States and Puerto Rico and give her products free access to our markets."

Hopeful of a generous economic policy, Root turned next to plans to terminate the military regime in the island. What sort of self-government should be granted? Were the inhabitants entitled to all the rights of American citizens? Should Puerto Rican institutions be made to conform to Anglo-Saxon ideals? The secretary favored maintaining, where possible, traditional customs. He would apply automatically only those safeguards for individuals that were contained in the Bill of Rights. On home rule, he was cautious. He devised a highly centralized system with virtually no popular participation. A governor and a legislative council were to be appointed by the President. Natives might sit on the council, but they would be in a minority. No elective assembly was envisaged. Root justified the absence of democratic features on the ground that a wise exercise of the ballot could not be expected from a population of which 90 per cent were illiterate.

McKinley concurred in this judgment and recommended Root's scheme to Congress.

On April 12, 1900, the President signed the Foraker Act, which fixed the relations between Puerto Rico and the United States for the rest of Root's term and, in some instances, down to 1917. Root had a hand in preparing this organic law, but on two points his wishes were disregarded. The Senate insisted upon more home rule and set up an elective lower house that would form, with the appointive council, a bicameral legislature. The House, for its part, held out for a temporary tariff on imports at rates approximately 15 per cent of the Dingley levies.

Root's reaction to these changes exposed him to the charge of subordinating enlightened policy to party unity. On the first, he was silent, although he obviously believed the islanders were unready to elect their own legislators. On the second, which flew in the face of the President's reference to "our plain duty," he was unhappy but did not publicly object. The Puerto Rican tariff split the Republican party wide open at the very time the administration was under heavy attack for its needless concessions to Britain in the first Hay-Pauncefote Treaty and for its correct but unpopular hands-off policy toward the Boers. Root regarded the uproar as a tempest in a teapot since the tariff would expire in fifteen months and since the money collected would be used in the island. He was willing to defend the President's shift on the ground that free trade in the Foraker Act might set an unfortunate precedent for dealing with the Philippines, but he also believed the episode could have been handled more wisely. To his critics, however, he seemed inconsistent and to lack the courage of his convictions.

With the end of military rule on May 1, 1900, the secretary's interest slackened. The new civil governor reported to the President through the Secretary of State, and by the end of 1901 the number of troops in the island had been drastically reduced. Root contributed less to the development of Puerto Rico than he did to that of Cuba and the Philippines; yet with Senator Joseph B. Foraker and Major General George W. Davis, the last military governor, he shares the credit and the blame for the organic law that remained relatively unchanged until 1917. In this, his first attempt to formulate a colonial policy, he revealed a realistic but conservative attitude toward insular self-government.

2. Cuba: A Pledge Redeemed

While Congress was putting the final touches on the Foraker Act, Root sailed for Cuba, where the situation was more complicated than in Puerto Rico. A crusade to free Cuba had been the primary cause of the appeal to arms in 1898, but by the Teller Amendment to the war resolution Congress specifically disclaimed any intention to annex the island to the United States, and the peace treaty had provided for only temporary American occupation.

Root contended that while the United States controlled Cuba, it was bound to prepare the island for self-government and to establish the basic relations for the future. The occupying authority, he thought, was obligated to quell disorder and to install a civil government of trained Cubans. Politically, Cuba must be a going concern when the United States withdrew. Furthermore, American rule must be maintained until effective guarantees had been secured for the fair treatment of American citizens. Strategically and economically, Cuba was too vital to the welfare of the United States to permit either European domination or discrimination by the Cubans.

Secondary matters, however, claimed immediate attention. Cuba escaped the devastating hurricane of August 1899, but it still bore the ravages of war when Root took office. The island needed cleaning up; and sanitation projects, road construction and school building — all soon to be hallmarks of American colonial rule — were well launched during the occupation. Root also found that Military Governor Major General John R. Brooke was not adequate for the job at hand; within five months he had replaced him with Brigadier General Leonard Wood. Wood's regime became a model for all future proconsuls.

Under Root's direction, Wood made preparations between April and September 1900 for a convention to frame the first Cuban constitution. The secretary exerted influence indirectly at two points. In voting for the delegates, he restricted the franchise. Root was bothered by the high proportion of Cuban illiteracy; and he confined the ballot to property holders, members or veterans of the Cuban army, and males who could read. He also insisted that the constitution contain a statement on the future relations between the United States and Cuba. Ostensibly, Root wanted to make sure that America's crusade had not been in vain and that its position vis-à-vis the island would be no worse than it had been in 1898. Actually, if his stipulations, as outlined in a letter to Hay on January 11, 1901, were met, the Cuban republic would be something less than independent and the authority of the United States rather more than it had been before the war.

Root's wishes prevailed. A further exposition in a letter to Wood, dated February 9, 1901, together with certain additions made by Congress, became the Platt Amendment to the Army Appropriation Act of March 2, 1901. Five of the eight conditions embodied in this far-reaching law, named after Senator Orville H. Platt, were Root's, though one had been changed, to the detriment of the

Cubans. The four unaltered articles limited the size of the public debt, validated the acts of the military government, assured the United States of the opportunity to buy or lease naval sites in specified areas, and prohibited Cuba from impairing by treaty its independence or permitting foreign colonization on its soil. The right of the United States to intervene to preserve that independence and to maintain a stable government was taken from Root's letter, but without his emphasis that the right was derived from the settlement with Spain, not from a grant by the Cuban people. Of the three new points, the most important required that the terms of the Platt Amendment be incorporated in a formal treaty with the United States as well as in the Cuban constitution.

The convention balked for a time before accepting the Platt Amendment. Many members regarded it as an infringement of sovereignty; others disliked specific phrases. Root combined firmness with persuasion to gain his goal. He made it clear that there would be no termination of military rule until the law was agreed to. He gave explicit assurances, on the other hand, that the right to intervene did not carry with it the license to meddle in the internal affairs of the island; and he promised that nothing short of a recurrence of the condition of 1898 would ever bring about American action.

The eventual acceptance of the Platt Amendment hastened the end of American occupation. To the amazement of the entire world, the United States, on May 20, 1902, redeemed its pledge and withdrew from the island. It left behind a record that has been praised by the most ardent champions of Cuban independence. Physically, economically, politically, and diplomatically, Cuba was stronger than at any time in its history.

Any judgment on Root's Cuban policy must be based upon an appreciation of the conditions under which it was formulated. As with other phases of Root's colonial administration, time has dimmed the luster of his achievement. The Platt Amendment, at first a source of strength for Cuba, eventually became a symbol of inferiority. It was framed in one diplomatic era and abrogated in another. As Root observed in 1934, "You cannot understand the Platt Amendment unless you know something about the character of Kaiser Wilhelm the Second." He might have added "and the changing Caribbean policy of the United States." The arrangement of 1901 was not unreasonable in its day. Its major flaw, as events proved, was that it inevitably bruised the pride of many Cubans. But although Root and his colleagues withheld complete independence from the infant republic, they did redeem a pledge that a cynical world had refused to take seriously.

3. *The Philippines: War and Peace*

By far the most annoying and persistent matter confronting the Secretary of War was the restoration of peace in the Philippines and their preparation for self-government. The difficulty and complexity of this problem can be attributed generally to the remoteness of the archipelago, differences in customs, language and legal traditions, mutual ignorance, and the tense international situation in the Far East. More specifically one can point to the unexpectedness of annexation, the widespread opposition in the United States to the step, and the ardent desire of most Filipinos for immediate independence — a desire that took the form of a bloody, three and a half-year insurrection against American rule.

The wholly unlooked for decision by McKinley to retain the islands made such a revolt likely, if not inevitable.

The men who had rebelled against Spain in 1896 believed that Dewey's invasion was designed to end Spanish sovereignty, not substitute American control. The Teller Amendment on Cuba gave substance to this assumption of disinterestedness. Indiscreet remarks by consular agents and unguarded statements by military officers further misled the Filipinos about the intentions of an administration that did not make up its own mind until the end of October 1898. Petty quarrels and suspicions among American and native troops around Manila, after its capture in August 1898, provided the spark that finally set off the conflagration on the night of February 4–5, 1899.

When Root took office, the insurrection had lasted almost six months and the end was not in sight. The secretary accepted the administration's contention that the uprising was the result of the ambition and bad faith of Emilio Aguinaldo and other native leaders. Root was concerned, however, not with recriminations and explanations, but with preventing the disintegration of American armed strength in the islands. As of February 1899, some 21,000 troops, regular and volunteer, had landed on Luzon. This force, utterly inadequate to cope with the far-flung archipelago, would soon dwindle to 3700, when the ratification of the peace treaty entitled to discharge those who had signed up in 1898. Fortunately, Congress had on March 2, 1899, authorized a new volunteer force of 65,000. The War Department's primary task in 1899 was to raise this new army, officer and train it, transport it halfway around the world, and at the same time bring back and disband its predecessor. All this was to be done when the science of logistics was in its infancy, at a time when McKinley's policy was undergoing increasing criticism, and in the face of a sullen and aroused population that was eager to hurl the foreigner into the sea.

Root's astounding success in stripping down one army in

the Philippines and building another in its place clearly revealed that Algerism was a thing of the past. By November 1899, when the end of the rainy season permitted launching a major offensive, American troops numbered 47,000. By January 1900, the total had reached 65,000, and by the close of that year, 74,000. The means for crushing organized opposition had been provided.

With sufficient manpower available, Root turned next to its efficient employment. By the late summer of 1899, there was considerable complaint against Major General Elwell S. Otis, military governor and commander of the 8th Army Corps. Stubborn, unbending and a glutton for detail, the bewhiskered Otis was the most controversial figure in a controversial episode. Lacking the glamor and personal magnetism of some of his subordinates, tied by his combined military and civil duties to his headquarters in Manila, and unwilling to delegate authority in the field to others, Otis was savagely attacked as incompetent. McKinley and Root, however, refused to yield to popular clamor and their faith was eventually justified.

In November 1899, with the rains over and the army rebuilt, Otis launched a three-pronged drive against the rebel forces on Luzon. While Major General Arthur Mac-Arthur pushed northward with one division along the railroad from San Fernando to Dagupan and Major General Henry W. Lawton led another division along a parallel route to cut off retreat to the east, Major General Loyd Wheaton landed an amphibious expedition on November 7 at San Fabian on Lingayen Gulf. Although this pincers movement failed to prevent, as intended, Aguinaldo's taking refuge in the mountain fastnesses, it did mark the end of organized resistance in northern Luzon. By early 1900 the insurrection passed into the stage of guerrilla activity and continued as such for another two years.

During the sporadic fighting that persisted in the islands

until July 1902, both sides committed vile atrocities. Fully appreciating the army's difficult task, Root was slow — too slow to please most reformers and humanitarians at home — to investigate cases of cruelty. He was much quicker to defend the honor of the American soldier waging an unprecedented and exasperating war in the tropics, and for the most part his defense was justified. For it, he was loved by the service as few civilian secretaries have ever been loved. But his stand also made his name anathema to the anti-imperialists and to many mugwump Republicans in New England.

With the coming of peace to the Philippines, the secretary moved to terminate military rule. Before Root's entry into the cabinet, McKinley had sent a commission, headed by President Jacob G. Schurman of Cornell University, to investigate conditions on the spot. Root said little during 1899, but listened quietly to those who had been in the islands, people like Senator Albert J. Beveridge, Admiral George Dewey, and Bishop Henry C. Potter. He omitted from his annual report in November all discussion of governmental questions and awaited instead the findings of Schurman's group. That body declared on January 31, 1900, that the islanders were not ready for self-rule and that the more intelligent inhabitants did not desire immediate independence. These conclusions were, at least, open to question.

On March 16 McKinley appointed a second commission with Circuit Judge William H. Taft as chairman. The instructions to this Second Philippine Commission, dated April 7, 1900, were written by Root. They directed the members to continue the work already commenced of organizing civil government and, as of September 1, 1900, to take over all legislative functions of the military regime. Root foresaw, however, a difficult transition period and urged close co-operation with the commanding general.

He advised that local customs be respected where possible. Most important of all, the secretary made clear that the fundamental liberties of individuals, embodied in the Bill of Rights, would be extended to the new colony.

In the next months, Root did what he could to obtain Congressional sanction for the commission's work. He was rewarded with the Spooner Amendment to the Army Appropriation Act of March 2, 1901. As with the Platt Amendment, which was appended to the same statute, Root had a hand in the document that bears Senator John C. Spooner's name. It seems likely that he wrote the first paragraph in which the executive was empowered to substitute civil for military rule. He was also responsible for a proviso which reserved the right to alter, amend, and repeal all franchises granted under the act. The Spooner Amendment was only a temporary grant of authority to the President until a more permanent law could be passed, but it enabled Root and his associates to proceed with the curtailment of army domination in the pacified areas. On July 4, 1901, Taft was installed as the first civil governor.

The death of McKinley in September 1901 did not alter the developing Philippine policy. Roosevelt, like his predecessor, had implicit faith in Root and Taft; and his close friend Henry Cabot Lodge had charge of the Senate committee that dealt with the islands. A concerted move during the winter of 1901-1902 to secure permanent legislation, however, met with several obstacles. A pending tariff proposal had already divided the administration's supporters, as it had in the case of Puerto Rico. The floor leaders in the Senate and House disagreed on the wisdom of creating an elective lower house. Lodge's committee was compelled to hold extended hearings from January 31 to June 28 on what began as testimony for framing the new law and ended as a wholesale anti-imperialist attack upon the record of the army in the Philippines. Finally, as the

spring wore on, Congressmen became much more excited
about the bill to select a route for the isthmian canal than
about the statute for the government of the Philippines. It
was something of a triumph that Root obtained any law at
all.

The organic act, approved July 1, 1902, perpetuated
and gave Congressional sanction to much of what Root
had done. The Taft commission was continued with its
chairman as civil governor (soon to be renamed governor
general), its individual members as heads of the executive
departments, and its collective membership as the upper
chamber of a bicameral legislature. Provision was made
for a lower house, to be chosen by popular vote; but this
assembly did not come into being immediately. All previous acts of the commission were approved, and Root's
instructions of 1900 were specifically endorsed. The protection of personal liberties that Root had insisted upon
was thus carried over into the new regime.

The pattern of administration thus set up was not drastically changed until the advent of Woodrow Wilson in
1913. It was, as in Puerto Rico, a conservative one. Under
Root, American colonial rule stressed material and physical well-being. Roads were built, sanitation introduced,
and education expanded. Responsible and intelligent
governors were selected. Economic enterprise was stimulated; but the dependencies were developed for the benefit of their inhabitants, not for the profit of absentee corporate interests.

This Rootian scheme has been criticized for its undemo-
cratic character. Self-rule was introduced slowly at first,
and this was wise. But the promise of ultimate enlarge-
ment was not very concrete. Neither territorial government, eventual statehood, nor outright independence was
included as the goal in Root's program. Nor did he modify
his views as the years passed. Like Taft, Wood, and his

other Republican collaborators, he was reluctant, even after a decade, to change the system established during 1899–1902. When Wilson's party proposed new legislation after 1913, Root seemed to regard the democratic potentialities of the islanders in the same conservative way he had done at the turn of the century. Stability, cleanliness, good roads, new schools, economic benefits, and responsible governors — these things the insular possessions received from Root in abundance. But representative institutions were granted sparingly, and the promise of freedom was absent.

4. The Army: Reorganization and the General Staff

With the colonial system established by mid-1902, the Secretary of War was free to concentrate upon a long overdue reorganization of the army. Never able to give the matter his undivided attention, Root had been compelled until then to proceed upon a piecemeal basis. Now, with the firm support of Roosevelt, he moved swiftly to modernize an institution which, in some respects, was little changed from the days of George Washington or John C. Calhoun.

First on Root's agenda was manpower. How large a regular army did a new world power require? In the two decades before the Cuban crisis, the authorized strength never exceeded 28,000 officers and men. During the war with Spain a force of 275,000 regulars and volunteers was provided for. To suppress the Filipino Insurrection, Congress set an aggregate of 100,000, and these were none too many to do the job.

In seeking to determine a reasonable size for the peacetime army, Root made it clear that the nation could not return to prewar levels. A force of 28,000, he pointed out in November 1900, would, in view of the country's growth, be proportionately only a third of what had prevailed in 1870. He asked, therefore, and obtained in February 1901 a minimum of about 60,000 enlisted men and a maximum of 100,000. During the remainder of his term Root did not take advantage of this flexibility, but was content to maintain the smaller figure.

A second change was the abolition of permanent assignments to staff jobs in Washington. The armed forces have always been plagued by the dilemma of securing skilled uniformed administrators to supervise procurement, supply, and records without dulling the fighting edge of the men performing those tasks. Competence at a desk or before a Congressional committee does not always carry with it competence in the field or before the enemy's defenses. To prevent those detailed to the department from losing touch completely with the line, without at the same time impairing the efficiency of the staff work, was a knotty problem.

Root sought to strike a proper balance between the conflicting needs of combat and administration. After prodding Congress for two years, he received in February 1901 the authority to substitute temporary for permanent detail. Appointment to staff positions in Washington was henceforth to be made from line officers for a period of four to five years, after which the incumbent must return to the troops for at least twelve months. To insure that the men thus assigned would be properly qualified for supervisory tasks, Root urged that all such appointments be decided on the basis of work completed at special service schools or at the new war college.

The third item in Root's program flowed logically from the second. It consisted of overhauling existing educational facilities and creating an Army War College. This last would be responsible for all instruction in the military establishment, would advise the Commander in Chief on a variety of subjects, and would offer courses on top-level planning and strategy. The navy had benefited from such a postgraduate school at Newport since 1884, but it was not until Root signed an order on November 27, 1901, that the army gained its counterpart in Washington, Simultaneously, the secretary acted to rehabilitate the special service schools — infantry, cavalry, artillery, and engineers — that had virtually been shut down during the war and insurrection for want of teachers and students. They were not only expanded for peacetime needs, but also thrown open to officers of the National Guard, former members of the volunteers, and graduates of private military colleges.

The fourth of Root's objectives was to breathe new life into the antiquated militia system. Opening the service schools to the National Guard only scratched the surface of the perennial problem of how to insure the instantaneous availability of an adequate body of trained reservists. The federal nature of our government and a universal prejudice against standing armies had conspired to place the primary responsibility in the hands of the states, with a consequent lack of standards and concern for the nation as a whole. Vested interests had long fought change, and no truly new legislation had been enacted since 1792

Root did not expound his ideas on this explosive subject until late in 1901, when the volunteers raised for duty in the Philippines had been demobilized. He did not then urge the abolition of the dual system but rather closer integration. He recommended that state units be given the same organization, equipment, and discipline as the regulars, but that the latter specialize in those branches of war-

fare requiring the most intensive and technical preparation. He proposed periodic joint exercises and instruction,
the expenses of which would be borne by the War Department. He set the number of reservists needed at between
250,000 and 300,000. Not until January 21, 1903, did
Congress yield to his pleas and declare the National Guard
to be the organized militia; not until March 2, 1903, did it
appropriate $2,000,000 to effect these changes.

By all odds the most far-reaching of Root's innovations
was the introduction of the general staff principle. Ever
since the War of 1812, the apex of the military hierarchy
had been defective. In time of war the role of the highest-
ranking officer, known as the commanding general, was
clear. He led the troops in the field or directed their de-
ployment from behind the front. In time of peace, however, he usually had his headquarters in Washington,
where he found that overlapping authority brought him
into conflict on the one hand with the civilian secretary
and on the other with the heads of the administrative departments, such as the adjutant general and the quarter-
master general. This last class of official, benefiting from
permanent staff assignments and from close ties with members of Congress, had been able to carve out little empires
which were often independent of their titular superior and
sometimes of the secretary himself.

To Root there were two cardinal principles of military
administration. One was civilian supremacy; the other was
power with responsibility. On both counts the anomalous
position of the commanding general offended his orderly
mind. But even more disturbing was the fact that no one
within the military establishment was directly charged to
study strategy and logistics. As he told the Senate in March
1902, "Neither law nor custom places the preparation of
plans for national defense in the hands of any particular officer or body of officers, and what is everybody's

business is nobody's business." To fill this vacuum, to fix the responsibility for top-level planning, and to end once and for all the ambiguous status of the ranking officer of the army, Root developed his plan for a General Staff Corps.

Under the Root scheme, the title of commanding general would be abolished when the existing incumbent retired in August 1903. Thereafter all orders would be issued in the name of the secretary, whose authority flowed from the President in his capacity as Commander in Chief of the armed forces. The secretary would act through a new officer known as the Chief of Staff. This man would not necessarily be, in fact he would rarely be, the senior officer in point of service or the field commander in time of war. Administratively, however, the bureau chiefs would report to him. His primary duty was to prepare plans for the national defense, maintain readiness, insure speedy mobilization, and, generally, advise the secretary on all military matters. To assist him in these tasks some forty or fifty officers, ranging from generals to captains, were detailed from the line for a term of four years. This group was called the General Staff Corps.

The obstacles to securing Congressional sanction for this fifth item in Root's program seemed insuperable. The proposed centralization of authority hit long-standing vested interests, particularly the quasi-independent bureau chiefs. It also appeared to be aimed at Commanding General Nelson A. Miles, a popular figure among Congressmen and veterans' organizations. Nursing political ambitions and completely unsympathetic to the McKinley-Roosevelt-Root policies, Miles resorted to fair means and foul in leading the uniformed opposition. Since Root had adapted some of his ideas from the German General Staff, he had to face also the cry of "Prussian militarism," already a term of opprobrium. The secretary bided his time and in December 1901, with Roosevelt's hearty endorsement, he began the final drive. Not until February 14, 1903, however, could the President sign what Newton D. Baker, a later civilian head of the army, described after Root's death as "the outstanding contribution made by any Secretary of War from the beginning of history."

Comprehensive as were Root's reforms, he did not tackle every problem or win every battle. He was blocked in his efforts to consolidate some of the supply agencies and to make sure that merit, not seniority, be given greater weight in promoting officers. Tactical reorganization of the field troops had to await Secretary Henry L. Stimson in 1912, while a more thorough overhauling of the department proper, as distinct from the high command, was delayed still longer. Co-operation with the navy was rather ineffectual while John D. Long, later an outspoken critic of the General Staff, ruled the admirals. After Long retired in May 1902, Root worked closely with William H. Moody, a warm personal friend; but their establishment in July 1903 of a Joint Army-Navy Board still left much to be desired.

Even the General Staff was not the immediate success that some of Root's uncritical admirers have depicted. The corps was burdened with unanticipated administrative duties and the old duplication of functions continued. A constant flow of officers from the staff to the line and back was not always attained. A long period of building and experimentation lay ahead.

Despite these qualifications, Root's record was one of outstanding achievement. Confronted with the increased importance of the military in the nation's life and the beginnings of a revolution in the technology of warfare, Root insisted upon civilian supremacy, a sympathetic understanding of the professional soldier, a logical command relationship, and ceaseless planning of strategy and logistics by those of proved competency. Hence there is still validity in Lord Haldane's oft-quoted remark of 1906, that in Root's five annual reports are to be found "the very last word concerning the organization and place of an army in a democracy."

By the end of 1902, Root began to think of resigning from the cabinet. His wife's distaste for Washington society was the chief reason, but other factors were at work. He had completed the task McKinley had summoned him to do. A colonial policy had been formulated and its administration established. The logic of events had led to an extensive reorganization of the army, and Congressional authorization for the last part of his program was in sight. On February 14, 1903, the very day he signed the General Staff Corps bill, Roosevelt wrote disconsolately to Taft, "The worst calamity that could happen to me officially is impending because Root tells me that he will have to leave me next fall." On February 1, 1904, Root resigned.

The genuine sorrow voiced by administration leaders revealed the importance Root had rapidly assumed in national politics. Virtually unknown in 1899, he had become the strong man in two successive cabinets. Aside from his dual duties as colonial administrator and civilian head of the army, he had several times acted in Hay's illness as Secretary of State, notably during the Boxer uprising in 1900. When in 1901 McKinley was shot, Root held steady the reins of office until the Vice-President could take over. When in 1902 the stubbornness of management in the anthracite strike threatened to plunge the nation into economic disaster, Root persuaded J. P. Morgan to bring the operators to their senses. When in 1903 England agreed to submit the vexing Alaskan boundary dispute to a mixed tribunal of outstanding jurists, Root was chosen as one of the three American representatives. In December 1899 he declined second place on the Republican ticket for

1900, alleging that he preferred to finish the job he had just begun. Had he decided otherwise, an assassin's bullet would have elevated him, not Roosevelt, to the Presidency.

"You know how much, how very much, Elihu has been to me," wrote Roosevelt to Mrs. Root on February 1, 1904. "I shall never have, and can never have, a more loyal friend, a more faithful and wiser adviser; nor will the government ever be served by any man with greater zeal, efficiency and success." The less ebullient but equally affectionate Hay declared in August 1903, "You stand today at the head of our public men. Anything you want is at your disposition. The only trouble is to find a place big enough for you." His successor, Taft, confided glumly to a friend, "Following Secretary Root . . . leaves me no opportunity to distinction as secretary of war. All I can do is merely to follow . . . his footsteps." The undemonstrative Lodge apologized for not coming to the station to say good-by, "because I hate partings when my feelings are engaged." After citing Root's many successes, the Senator concluded: "To have a man who has done such really great things retire in the prime of his powers is a sore loss. . . . It is all the more to be deplored because in all this brilliant service I have never seen more complete disinterestedness. . . . Our friendship I am sure cannot be dimmed or fade because we live in different cities. But . . . I do not like to feel that I can no longer see you every day and any day I want to."

Not all Americans shared these sentiments. To pacifists, the foes of expansion, and the friends of the Filipinos, Root represented everything that was abhorrent in the colonial adventure. Veterans never forgave the public reprimand Root had delivered to Miles in 1901, while Democrats never forgot his devastating attack on Bryan in the campaign of 1900. So bitter were certain anti-imperialistic mugwumps on the Board of Overseers of Harvard University that they blocked for several years the award to him of an honorary degree.

As Secretary of War, Root exemplified constructive conservatism at its best. In no other period of his public career did his talents for creative planning and efficient administration have freer scope. His keen analysis of men and measures, his realistic appraisal of what was attainable, his reliance on judicial procedures, his insistence that change be orderly and with due regard for existing institutions and interests, and finally, his balancing power with responsibility were all fully disclosed. Shortcomings inevitably appeared in his labors; but they were ones that the passing of time and a later generation, with a different outlook and another standard of judgment, would emphasize.

I I I

World Politics:

Secretary of State   1905-1909

ROOT'S RETIREMENT from public life was more apparent than real. To be sure, he held no official position from February 1, 1904, until July 7, 1905. During that time he reassumed his old leadership of the New York bar and engaged in a lucrative practice that netted annually more than $100,000 — a vivid contrast to his government salary of $8000. But the Root of 1904 could not pick up the kind of life he had led before 1899. He was a national political figure; and even when busy with the law, his thoughts reverted to his strenuous friend in the White House.

The persistence of close ties with Roosevelt in this interim explains Root's sudden return to high office. The President continued to look to Root for assistance, and he did not look in vain. In February 1904, the former Secretary of War delivered two staunch defenses of Roosevelt before the Union League Clubs of New York and Chicago; in these he helped to demolish the last opposition to the colonel's renomination. In June he served as temporary chairman of the Republican National Convention, and his keynote speech acclaimed the foreign and colonial policies of the McKinley and Roosevelt administrations. During the ensuing campaign, Root contributed generously from his own pocket, secured funds from others, and took the stump himself in the East. All the time he kept in touch with the White House. He repeatedly scrutinized and criticized drafts of Presidential utterances and frequently amused Roosevelt by his wit. In greeting his former chief on the eve of re-election in 1904, Root wrote: "I congratulate you on attaining the respectable age of 46. You have made a good start in life and your friends have great hopes for you when you grow up."

During these eighteen months attempts were made to lure Root back on to the public stage. He refused, however, to succeed Mark Hanna as chairman of the Republican National Committee; and he would not yield to pleas, even from Roosevelt and Lodge, that he run for governor of New York and thus make sure of that state in 1904. Had Root consented and been elected, he would have become the most likely successor to Roosevelt in 1908.

Then on July 1, 1905, John Hay died. For several reasons Roosevelt turned instinctively to Root. First, he had more respect and, barring Lodge, greater affection for Root than for any public man. Second, Root was Hay's own choice. Two years earlier, the ailing Secretary of State had begged to be allowed to resign so that Root could be persuaded to stay in the cabinet. But most of all, Root was the logical selection. Of the possibilities mentioned in the press, Spooner and Joseph H. Choate were unacceptable to the President, while Lodge preferred to remain in the Senate. Taft, who had followed Root in the War Department and had been Acting Secretary of State in the spring of 1905, would have been an excellent appointment; but by naming Root, Roosevelt obtained the aid of both strong men. As for Root's competency in foreign affairs, he had helped shape China policy in 1900, had foreshadowed the Roosevelt Corollary in the Platt Amendment of 1901, had sat on the Alaskan Boundary Tribunal in 1903, and had spoken extensively on all phases of the subject during the campaign of 1904.

To Roosevelt's surprise and delight, Root accepted the bid with alacrity and enthusiasm. What prompted his decision is not wholly clear; but affection for Roosevelt, loyalty to Hay, and a sense of public duty must have figured prominently in his thinking. It is possible that he missed the excitement of Washington and that he saw new opportunities for usefulness that had been closed to him a year and a half before. One thing, however, is certain. Despite newspaper allegations, there was no bargain involved, no arrangement whereby Roosevelt promised to back Root for the Presidency in 1908 if he returned as Secretary of State in 1905. Root had no illusions about his own availability for the Chief Magistracy, while the President was to waver for another two years before reluctantly supporting Taft rather than Root.

1. *The Nature of Root's Diplomacy*

When Root entered the State Department, the nation still felt the effect of the revolution in its foreign policy seven years before. McKinley's decision to retain the Philippines had projected the United States into the arena of world politics, thus hastening a development which the phenomenal growth in population, industry, fluid capital, and military might during the late nineteenth century had rendered inevitable. For better or for worse, the United States had become inextricably entwined in the shifting global balance of power. Old friends loomed as potential rivals; traditional enemies were found pursuing parallel courses.

But the immediate problems of 1905 were not those of

1898. The popular mood had changed. A colonial policy had been formulated, a canal site had been acquired, an interest in preserving a unified China with equality of commercial opportunity had been proclaimed, and a policeman's role in the Caribbean had been assumed. By 1905 the American people were less jingoistic, less eager for adventure amid palm and pine, and more aware of the implications of their decisive action of 1898. Although there was to be no turning back, a sober second thought presaged more realism and less emotion in diplomacy. As Secretary of State, Root was nothing if not realistic.

During his term, Root did not alter the fundamental character of the foreign policy of the United States. He left behind no basic principle, no familiar doctrine; and the single agreement that bears his name was not wholly of his making. Certainly, he did not undertake to enact any comprehensive program. Yet Root ranks today among the three or four ablest Secretaries of State in American history, a judgment Roosevelt would amend to read "the ablest."

"The main object of diplomacy," wrote Root on September 9, 1905, is "to keep the country out of trouble." Accordingly, he avoided unnecessary drama and stimulated crises. His legal career had trained him to conciliate, not antagonize, to seek reasonable solutions, not spectacular triumphs. He never forgot that, under the Constitution, the conduct of foreign relations is entrusted jointly to the executive and the legislature and that on some matters the demarcation of jurisdiction is blurred. Root had an ability to get along with people of all types, and he was the first incumbent to treat South American diplomats as the equals of Europeans.

Like every Secretary of State, Root's success depended not only upon his own ideas and his handling of foreign representatives but also upon his relations with the President, the Senate, and his own department.

The problem affecting the President was whether the Secretary of State leads or follows. Between Roosevelt and Root there was no question of one dominating the other. Both men were too independent and strong-willed to play a subordinate role; each loved and admired his associate. To be sure, during Hay's long illness, the President had grown accustomed to acting as his own Secretary of State; and it cannot be denied that he enjoyed himself. But with the coming of Root, he mended his ways and the result was a fruitful collaboration. In some matters Roosevelt was the originator; in others, Root. By nature the former was more active and impulsive; Root's was usually, though not always, the restraining hand. Essential to this harmonious relationship was mutual understanding and Root's utter lack of political ambition. He willingly yielded the limelight to his chief. Roosevelt, to his credit, fully recognized this disinterestedness and never tired of singing Root's praises.

Root was also immensely successful in getting along with the Senate. Here the problem was one of obtaining consent to treaties. Ever since the Civil War the upper house had manifested a growing disposition to block such agreements, either by inaction, amendment, or outright rejection. Hay was notoriously inept in dealing with that body; in 1905 Roosevelt frankly admitted that he sought in the new secretary a person who "will get along well with the Senate . . . and prevent the need of incessant amendment of treaties."

Root met this qualification admirably. In contrast to Hay before him and to Knox, Bryan, and Lansing afterward, he lost no important pact in the Senate. The secret of his success — aside from careful draftsmanship and a realistic appreciation of what was possible — was a conscious effort to cultivate the Senate. He always consulted with its leaders, especially those on the Foreign Relations Committee, in advance of his negotiations. He attended as many committee hearings as he was invited to. He mixed with the solons at social functions and was not above an occasional game of poker with the honorable legislators. Hence he succeeded where the brusque Olney, the sensitive Hay, the lazy Knox, or the intellectually superior Acheson would often fail.

Root also dealt skillfully with his own department. Here the problem was one of efficient administration and loyal support from his subordinates. Root combined in a happy proportion the ability to delegate work and to dig for himself. His keen, analytical mind enabled him to master quickly, as he had done in the War Department, the most complicated issues, while his gift for devising ingenious solutions shortened many tortuous negotiations. Root drew the best out of his assistant secretaries, the urbane but warmhearted Robert Bacon, the venerable but deaf Alvey A. Adee (a State Department fixture from 1878 to 1924), and the irascible but talented Huntington Wilson. He leaned heavily upon James B. Scott, who became solicitor in January 1906, and upon Chandler P. Anderson, who had begun as special counsel the previous year.

Surprisingly enough, in view of his reorganization of the army, Root instituted very few administrative changes in a department desperately in need of reform. His most important accomplishment was a bill to improve the consular service, which he and Lodge steered through Congress in April 1906. A boon to future historians was the start he made in modernizing the archaic filing system in use since 1789. Ten months before leaving office, Root begrudgingly accepted Wilson's advice and set up a Division of Far Eastern Affairs; but a fuller breakdown into geographic desks had to await Secretary Philander C. Knox, who made Wilson his first assistant.

2. The Contribution to World Peace

In 1905 both Root and Roosevelt believed, as most Americans still did not, that as a world power the United States had a stake in world peace. War anywhere on the globe might upset the existing balance of power and thus affect the national interest and security. To make this belief part of American foreign policy was the aim of both men. In realizing that end, they had an equal share.

Roosevelt's contribution came first and was the more spectacular. Between May and August 1905, by skillful use of good offices and mediation, he brought to a close the Russo-Japanese War and, almost simultaneously, helped to avert, by arranging an international conference at Algeciras, a European conflagration over Morocco. For his peacemaking at Portsmouth, Roosevelt received the Nobel Prize of 1906, the first American to be so honored. Six years later Root became the second American recipient. His award was based upon his contribution to the peace of the Western Hemisphere, to the cause of arbitration, and to the defense of the sanctity of treaties, as well as upon his earlier achievement in establishing an enlightened colonial system.

Although the most dangerous phase of the Moroccan controversy was over by the time Root began actual work on October 1, 1905, he had still to instruct the delegates, supervise their negotiations, and gain Senatorial consent to their labors. For while the American people might applaud a timely Presidential mediation between the armed camps of Europe, they might object to participation in a

conference dealing with the trade and stability of the
North African powder keg. Would not such a course en-
tangle the country in non-American affairs, a step warned
against by the Founding Fathers and zealously avoided ever
since? Root did not believe that the Farewell Address forbade throwing American influence on the side of world
peace, provided the United States assumed no obligation
to uphold the arrangement agreed upon. But to many citizens, attendance at the Algeciras Conference, which sat
from January 16 to April 7, 1906, and the subscription to
the General Act agreed upon there, constituted an unnecessary departure from the hallowed tradition of isolationism.

To forestall opposition in a Senate already aroused by
Roosevelt's innovations elsewhere, Root instructed the
American delegates to make a statement, on signing the
treaty, disclaiming for the United States any political interests in Morocco and any obligation to enforce the settlement. The Senators, however, were not satisfied by
this concession; and in conferring their approval on December 12, 1906, they appended a formal reservation
which declared that there was no intention to depart from
a traditional policy which prohibited participation in
political questions entirely European in scope. Root did
not favor the addition of such an explanation to the treaty,
but he accepted it to insure ratification.

Another opportunity to advance the cause of world
peace was presented to Root by the Second Hague Conference, which met from June 15 to October 18, 1907.
There the thorniest problem concerned the reduction and
limitation of armaments. The First Hague Conference in
1899 had failed dismally on that score, and prospects for
successful action grew bleaker with each passing year.
The continental powers were reluctant even to discuss
the matter; when the Tsar issued the new invitations,

he omitted mention of it. Great Britain doubted whether anything useful could be done in 1907, while the United States, regarding her own army as negligible and her navy as barely adequate for the new demands made upon it, felt that no sacrifice on her part was required. On the other hand, both Root and Roosevelt believed it would be psychologically unfortunate to ignore armaments altogether; and they reserved the right to bring the topic before the conference. After interminable preliminary conversations with the British, however, they adopted a policy which, in retrospect, shirked the issue. In his instructions of May 31, 1907, the secretary cautioned the delegates not to take the initiative but simply to support any proposal by another state to discuss the problem. No such suggestion was forthcoming, and the Americans acquiesced in the decision to do nothing, except recommend further study of the subject.

Toward other objectives Root made limited progress. The Porter Resolution, sponsored by the United States, forbade the use of force by one nation to collect contract debts owed its citizens by another. Designed to please the Latin Americans who, understandably, were sensitive on this point, the resolution fell somewhat short of its goal by permitting the employment of force if the debtor refused to arbitrate or, having arbitrated, failed to abide by the verdict. The doctrinaire Latins wanted to outlaw force under all circumstances; but neither the Europeans nor Root, eager as he was for hemispheric unity, were prepared to go that far. The partial solution, adopted at The Hague, was never formally approved by the home governments of the Latin American states.

The third important matter dealt with by Root at the conference was compulsory arbitration of international disputes. Here his efforts were along two lines. First, he sought to define the types of controversies most easily set-

tled by arbitration, which is the submission of a dispute between two or more nations to an individual, a commission
or a court for a final decision that is binding on all parties.
Once this definition had been worked out, Root hoped to
draft a general treaty that would require the Hague signatories to resort to arbitration in the future for those classes
of disputes. In 1907 only three quarters of the nations voting were willing to take this second step; and the final Convention for the Pacific Settlement of International Disputes, therefore, did not make arbitration obligatory. But
the margin seemed to Root so overwhelming and the idea
so worth while that, after the conference, he went ahead on
a less ambitious program of individual treaties with states
that felt as he did.

At The Hague, Root sought also to improve the arbitral
machinery already in existence. In 1899 the first conference had set up a Permanent Court of Arbitration, a rather
misleading name for a rather powerless body. The Hague
Court was not a tribunal that sat regularly, but only a
panel of some hundred individuals who could be called
upon to serve as arbitrators. These persons, most of whom
never received that call, were not always trained as jurists.
They were often diplomats or statesmen, and they tended
to decide cases not on legal principles but on grounds of
expediency. This practice of compromise, of splitting the
difference, irrespective of law and equity, made nations
with strong cases reluctant to resort to arbitration. Root
felt that the better way was to have a true court, small in
size, regularly in session, staffed by men imbued with the
juridical spirit.

In his instructions to the American delegates, Root
sketched the outlines of a permanent Court of Arbitral
Justice. His plan was enthusiastically received but failed of
adoption because of a single mechanical detail. How were
the judges to be chosen? On the vast panel of the Hague

Court every nation could have members; but the new tribunal, to be effective, had to be kept small and only a few states could be represented thereon at any one time. Neither Root nor the conferees could resolve this problem in 1907; and the proposed Court of Arbitral Justice, though endorsed in principle, had to wait until 1920 when, with the machinery of the League of Nations Council and Assembly available, it emerged as the World Court.

The meager accomplishments of the Second Hague Conference disappointed many peace advocates. Root, however, was not discouraged. Never a Utopian, he did not expect the battlements of Mars to crumble at a single bugle's blast. Nor was he surprised when the Senate, in its resolution of ratification, appended reservations reaffirming its control over specific arbitration agreements and its devotion to isolationism and the Monroe Doctrine.

Proof of Root's willingness to be content with small gains can be found in the twenty-four bilateral arbitration treaties that he negotiated between February 10, 1908 and January 23, 1909. Two of his predecessors, Olney in 1897 and Hay in 1904, had made similar attempts to obligate the United States to arbitrate certain types of disputes. On both occasions the Senate had interposed amendments altering the intent or the working of the agreements, and none of them had ever been ratified.

Roosevelt had been in the White House during Hay's negotiations, and he had backed his secretary's efforts to block all Senate amendments. He had been outraged when the legislators, including Lodge, had insisted upon a change that would require Senatorial approval for every subsequent agreement to arbitrate. It was ridiculous, he asserted in 1905, to sign a general arbitration treaty that did nothing more than say that arbitration treaties might be entered into in the future. When the upper chamber

stood firm, the President put the Hay treaties on the shelf
and refused to ask the other nations to accept the Senate's
terms.

One of Root's most impressive achievements was to secure within three years a virtual about-face by the President. The Senate amendment, which he had derided and
scorned in 1905, Roosevelt accepted, for all intents and
purposes, in 1908. To be sure, Root's careful wording enabled both the executive and the legislature to insist they
had yielded nothing; but in effect, the Senate's views prevailed and Root had to go out of his way to assure the President's friends that the new treaties did not constitute a
defeat for the administration.

The Root arbitration pacts of 1908–1909 provided that
differences of a legal nature and those relating to the interpretation of treaties, which could not be settled by ordinary diplomacy, would be referred to the Hague Court.
Disputes involving the vital interests, honor and independence of the contracting parties were exempted
from this compulsion. In each case the special agreement
defining the scope of the arbitration was to be approved by
a two-thirds vote of the Senate.

Some students of international law believe that the Root
treaties marked a backward rather than a forward step on
the road to the pacific settlement of international disputes. They cite not only the need for Senatorial consent in
each case but also the exemptions regarding vital interests, honor and independence. Any differences of consequence, they argue, could be placed in those broad cate-
gories. To such arguments Root replied, at the time and
afterward, that arbitration cannot cope with all contin-
gencies, that nations will never agree to entrust to it certain classes of disputes, and that if, in a moment of zeal
they do, they will break their word when a specific crisis
arises. Such a repudiation then, Root contended, would do

more harm to the cause of world peace than a refusal to sign the sweeping treaty in the first place.

The subsequent record of American diplomatic history has confirmed Root's judgment. Despite several attempts by the executive branch to frame a broader arbitral agreement, the Senate has never consented to go beyond the Root formula. And in 1908 that formula seemed a sufficient curtailment of a nation's freedom of action so that two major powers, Germany and Russia, declined to make such a treaty with the United States.

3. A Turning Point in the Far East

The entry of the United States into the arena of global politics in 1898 brought about a drastic shift in familiar attitudes and traditional policies toward other world powers. As a result of certain dramatic incidents during the war with Spain, Germany replaced England as the most likely enemy of the future. As a result of her reply to Hay's Open Door notes and of her tactics in Manchuria after the Boxer uprising, Russia lost the vague friendship bequeathed by Civil War myths and came to be regarded as the greatest single threat to American interests in China. Even Japan, a long-time protégé of the United States and the popular favorite in her clash with Russia in 1904–1905, was transformed by alarmists into a "yellow peril," when her criticism of Roosevelt's peacemaking at Portsmouth and the re-emergence of the immigration question on the Pacific slope produced in 1906 the nearest threat to war that occurred while Root was Secretary of State.

In general, Root reflected these shifting tides of opinion. Toward England he was uniformly cordial without gushing over, as Hay sometimes did. Toward Germany he continued to be as suspicious as he had been in April 1900, when he had publicly predicted that the Reich would soon challenge the Monroe Doctrine. For Russia he had only scorn and contempt, but he kept these emotions under a tighter rein than did either Roosevelt or Hay.

With Japan, Root was loath to abandon nineteenth-century sentimentalities. He hoped, even after 1905, that she would become the England of the Orient, with a constitutional form of government, a freedom from excessive territorial ambition, and a desire to promote stability and equality of commercial opportunity in a troubled area. Feeling as he did, he approved the renewal of the Anglo-Japanese alliance in 1905, accepted as inevitable and desirable the gradual absorption of Korea, and scouted the likelihood in his lifetime of a Japanese-American war.

In the relations with Japan during 1905–1909, Root played a lesser role than Roosevelt. With some matters he had nothing to do; with others his part was slight. Thus the negotiations leading to the peace at Portsmouth were completed before he actually took office. The Taft-Katsura agreement of July 29, 1905, on Korea and the Philippines, together with the President's approval of it, occurred while he was vacationing in Labrador. In the controversy precipitated by the San Francisco School Board's segregation order of October 1906, Roosevelt took personal charge; and it was he who decided in June 1907 to transfer the battle fleet from the Atlantic to the Pacific and then bring it back by circumnavigating the globe.

Root's specific contribution to lessening Japanese-American tensions during 1905–1909 was threefold. First, he helped negotiate the gentlemen's agreement which solved, for a time, the immigration irritant. The gentlemen's agreement was not a single diplomatic document but a series of notes exchanged between February 1907 and

February 1908 whereby Japan agreed herself to restrict the flow of coolie labor to the West Coast. Root adopted this indirect method because an outright exclusion law would have needlessly offended the Japanese and because a formal treaty could not be obtained quickly. Several persons on both sides of the Pacific had a hand in this accord, but it was Root's patience and sense of timing that insured success.

The gentlemen's agreement was, admittedly, not a perfect solution. Control over the problem was left to Japan. Congress resented this loss of authority, and the Senate henceforth made certain that controversies over immigration would not be submitted to arbitration or to any league of nations for settlement. Nor did the Japanese issue in California disappear after 1908. Yet the Root formula accomplished its main purpose without losing Nipponese good will, while the ill-advised Exclusion Act of 1924, which Root later deplored, dealt a damaging blow to friendly relations.

A second step Root took to promote amity with Japan was the arbitration treaty of May 5, 1908. That pact required arbitration in only certain types of disputes, and it did not cover controversies over immigration. But the mere act of signing, at a time when the United States concluded similar treaties with most of the other major powers, helped diminish mutual suspicion.

Root's final effort to clear the air of hostility was a joint declaration of policy in the Pacific. The Root-Takahira exchange of notes on November 30, 1908, was only an executive agreement and did not, therefore, bind Roosevelt's successors. In it the two governments affirmed their desire to encourage commerce in the Pacific, to maintain the *status quo* in that area, and to support by peaceful means the independence and territorial integrity of China, as well as equal opportunity for trade and industry therein.

They promised, further, to respect the possessions of each other in the Pacific region and to consult together in case the *status quo* or the principle of equality of opportunity were threatened.

The Root-Takahira agreement has been criticized as vague and confusing, as a blow to China, and as a surrender to Japan. The most frequently voiced objection is that the United States gave Tokyo a free hand in Manchuria in return for a pledge not to attack Hawaii or the Philippines. Actually, Root had no such bargain in mind. The broad terms in which he couched his ideas were intended to conciliate, not conceal. The secretary was not greatly bothered about Manchuria; that was to come later. Although he knew Japan could seize Oahu if she wished, he believed in November 1908 that Nippon harbored no aggressive designs against the United States. In 1907 she might have, but not in 1908.

Root was eager to leave office with some symbol of a restored Japanese-American cordiality. He was too realistic to assume that a mere paper agreement could restrain a Japan bent on conquest. But he trusted the existing regime in Tokyo, and he saw no harm and much good in a mutual subscription to general principles. Hence he accepted without quibbling the expansive clauses over which some scholars have pored as if they were a Biblical text. He sought a short-term gain, not a set of rules to last forever.

4. *The First Good Neighbor*

Root's most spectacular work as Secretary of State was the steps taken to promote hemispheric solidarity. The efforts to regain the good will of Latin America and to remove all friction with Canada and Newfoundland were peculiarly his own. Roosevelt exercised less influence and provided less supervision in these matters than in any other.

By 1905 the time was ripe for a fresh approach to the problems of the New World. For years the diplomats from the southern republics had been treated with condescension, if not disdain. Two other things had stored up a reservoir of dislike below the Rio Grande. One was the alleged "rape of Colombia" — Roosevelt's intervention in (some called it instigation of) the revolution on the isthmus in 1903. The other was the growing tendency of the United States to define the Monroe Doctrine in ever broader terms, to transform a declaration originally intended to prevent European interference in the domestic affairs of American nations into one to justify such interference by the United States itself.

When Root assumed charge of the State Department, the sensitive spot of the Western Hemisphere was the Caribbean. While the Panama Canal was being built, Washington looked with distrust at every European move in the lands washed by that sea and viewed with alarm every sign of instability that might encourage foreign intervention. Peace and order were the objectives of American policy in that area; and it was no coincidence that seven months before Root took office, Roosevelt had formulated his corollary to the Monroe Doctrine. This gloss on the principles of 1823 declared that chronic wrongdoing by American states or sheer impotence to discharge international obligations might compel the United States to exercise a police or supervisory power in order to forestall similar action by the European countries whose citizens were endangered or whose debt payments were being withheld.

The most pressing Caribbean problem confronting Root in 1905 grew out of Roosevelt's maladroit attempt to apply his corollary to the Dominican Republic. Chronic wrongdoing and impotence were manifested all too clearly in that turbulent island state, wracked by revolution and burdened by debt. Roosevelt was probably correct in assuming that it was best for all concerned — the islanders, the European creditors and the United States — to appoint an American collector of customs, who would divert the imposts from the pockets of native adventurers into a fund to service the national debt. Although the President shrewdly diagnosed the disease and prescribed the proper medicine, he erred in ministering to the patient. He tried first to do the job by an executive agreement; then, when the Senate understandably protested, he negotiated a treaty that was much more sweeping in its rights and obligations than the circumstances required. In March 1905, the Senate adjourned after refusing to vote on the pact; whereupon Roosevelt bypassed that body and instituted his control by a modus vivendi, or informal agreement, with the Dominican leaders.

Congress reassembled in December 1905 in a belligerent mood, but it now had to deal with a tactful Secretary of State. Within two years Root untangled the knotted threads in Santo Domingo and erected a customs control that satisfied almost everyone concerned. He did this by providing suspicious Senators with a full explanation of his purpose, by discouraging the landing of American troops without a prior Dominican request, and by negotiating a new treaty that markedly reduced both the obligations of the United States and the infringement of Dominican sovereignty. To this second treaty the Senate gave its approval on February 25, 1907.

Less in need of immediate attention, but more ominous for the future, was the unfinished business with Colombia growing out of Roosevelt's role in the Panama revolution of 1903. Part of this unfinished business was Colombia's demand for compensation for her "lost province." The rest had to do with establishing diplomatic relations between Colombia and Panama, adjusting boundaries, and straightening out the public debt. Roosevelt, of course, denied that the "bandits of Bogotá" were entitled to restitution and refused to arbitrate the matter. Root likewise believed that Colombia had no legal ground for grievance, but he was eager to restore amicable ties. Hence he grasped the opportunity in June 1906, when Colombia modified her demands and requested the good offices of the United States in its negotiations with Panama, to compose all outstanding problems affecting the isthmus.

It took Root thirty-one months to reach an accord. Not until January 9, 1909, could he obtain three interlocking treaties between the United States and Colombia, between the United States and Panama, and between Colombia and Panama. The details need not detain us; for, to Root's intense disappointment, the friendly Reyes regime in Bogotá was promptly overthrown and its successor rejected Root's terms. This denouement was the more regrettable because Root's adjustment was sounder than those subsequently arrived at by the Wilson and Harding administrations.

Root was not content simply to liquidate existing difficulties. He was determined to inaugurate a policy of the good neighbor. He did this in several different ways. One was to establish close personal friendships with certain Latin ministers in Washington. Another was to associate the United States and Mexico in joint efforts to preserve peace in Central America. A third was to secure New World representation at The Hague, first by obtaining a postponement of the second conference when it conflicted with an inter-American gathering in the summer of 1906, and, second, by drafting a plan which led to the attendance in 1907 of eighteen American states in contrast to the two which had been present in 1899. But the most enduring moves were his own South American tour of 1906 and his cosponsorship of the Central American Peace Conference of 1907.

The ostensible reason for Root's unprecedented good-will tour was to attend the Third Inter-American Conference that assembled at Rio de Janeiro on July 23, 1906. No previous Secretary of State, while in office, had ever been outside of the country; and no subsequent incumbent went to another such gathering until Cordell Hull journeyed to Montevideo in 1933. Root sailed from New York on the Fourth of July, touched at Puerto Rico and several Brazilian ports, addressed the conference on July 31, and then circumnavigated the continent, visiting on his way Uruguay, Argentina, Chile, Peru, Colombia, and Panama. His experiment had succeeded beyond his fondest hopes, Roosevelt was delighted, American commercial interests were ecstatic, and the Latins were flattered. Henceforth, his name would be coupled with those of Henry Clay and James G. Blaine as champions of hemispheric friendship.

While Root was promoting amity in the chancelleries of South America, the cauldron of war boiled over in the jungles of Central America. Sensitive to disorder in that region, Roosevelt in Root's absence enlisted the aid of Mexico to effect a temporary truce. Such joint action with the southern neighbor was dear to Root's heart. He not only approved what had been done but also repeated the stratagem in 1907, when fresh outbreaks occurred, by sponsoring with Mexico a conference at Washington to deal with Central America.

The Central American Peace Conference that sat from November 14 to December 20, 1907 was another manifestation of Root's determination to collaborate in every possible way with Mexico. It also established a new recognition policy, whereby the five Central American republics pledged themselves not to recognize any regime that came into power through revolution. The major achievement, however, was the Central American Court of Justice. The plan for this tribunal came from the fertile mind of Elihu Root in the very year his hopes for a world-wide body had been frustrated at The Hague. The Central American Court lasted in its original form until 1917, when Wilson and Lansing allowed themselves to be maneuvered into a position which led to the demise of the worth-while experiment.

While Root injected a new spirit into relations with Latin America, he successfully eliminated almost every source of friction with Canada. In wiping the slate clean, he was greatly aided by the complete understanding existing between him and Ambassador James Bryce, by his assiduous cultivation of Dominion leaders, and by the obvious eagerness of the British Foreign Office to keep on the best of terms with the Roosevelt administration. Since Root carefully avoided the delicate subject of commercial reciprocity upon which Hay before him and Knox after him came to grief, he encountered no real defeat. In his last nine months in office he signed five treaties and put all but the final touches on a sixth. The two most important were that of January 11, 1909, which set up a permanent joint commission to handle all controversies affecting boundary waters, and that of January 27, 1909, which, by reference to the Hague Court, laid to rest the perennial bickering over the Newfoundland fishing rights.

The years from 1905 to 1909 were probably the most enjoyable of Root's public life. As Secretary of State, he encountered fewer obstacles and less criticism than as Secretary of War. There was no Miles to bedevil him and no anti-imperialists to berate him. He also relaxed more in the spontaneous gaiety of the group that gathered around Roosevelt. It was then that the names of the musketeers were assumed, with Root as Athos, Secretary of War Taft as Porthos, Attorney General (later Associate Justice) Moody as Aramis, and the dashing, irrepressible President as D'Artagnan.

On January 27, 1909, Root retired, again at his own request. Although the Roosevelt administration had six weeks more to run, he wished to rest before commencing in March his new duties as United States Senator. Undoubtedly, he also wanted his loyal first assistant, Robert Bacon, to have the honor of serving as Secretary of State for a short period.

In his day, Root's diplomacy was deemed highly successful, and most historians share that contemporary estimate. If his achievements in the State Department appear less tangible than those in the War Department, it is because his work was often negative in character — preventing amendments to treaties in the Senate, curbing an impetuous chief, and keeping the country out of trouble. With Japan, he helped liquidate a serious crisis; and in the realm of world politics he revealed an international outlook which, however limited it may seem today, was advanced for his time.

For his trail-blazing role as the twentieth century's first good neighbor, Root deserves unstinted praise. Yet we must not exaggerate his accomplishments. The immediate results of the Rio Conference were, actually, slight; the attendance of the New World states at The Hague seemed to some people a mixed blessing; and the Colombian grievance, despite his best efforts, remained unappeased. The collapse of self-government in Cuba in September 1906 and the reluctant intervention by the United States that followed were personally embarrassing to Root, for they occurred as he was completing his good-will tour and reflected upon the thoroughness of his work for that island as Secretary of War.

An even bigger mistake would be to take Secretary Root

out of his time period. His thinking, at least so far as the Caribbean was concerned, was shaped by the configuration of forces in that area before the First World War. Distrust of Germany, irritation at debt-ridden republics whose chronic wrongdoing invited European interference, and, above all, the need for stability near the uncompleted canal — those ideas were paramount. Only by keeping them in mind can we understand Root's full acceptance of the Roosevelt Corollary, which has long since been abandoned by American diplomats, or his unbounded admiration for Porfirio Díaz, whose reputation has long since been tarnished by a social upheaval in Mexico after 1910.

The influence of Root's conservatism upon his work as Secretary of State is less evident than upon his labors as Secretary of War and United States Senator. His concern for efficient administration continued, but he did not attempt to reorganize the State Department or even the entire foreign service. In the Caribbean he strove for order and stability, demanding responsibility of those in power. Toward the restless Latins, however, he exhibited a patience that was absent in his dealings with the anti-imperialists on the one hand and with the progressives on the other. Regarding the momentous issue of isolationism, he was foremost among those who recognized that America's place in the world had changed; yet in conducting diplomacy in the new century, he was careful not to forsake old traditions too quickly. He placed his reliance on arbitration and international law to preserve the peace, rather than on a more ambitious league of states with quasi-legislative functions and with the power to use armed force.

I V
The Progressive Era:
United States Senator   1909-1915

IN MARCH 1909 Root began a term in the United States Senate that should have brought fresh laurels and formed a fitting climax to an outstanding public career. For his new tasks Root seemed superbly equipped. He possessed an intimate knowledge of both domestic and foreign affairs, a broad experience in handling diverse men and situations, a towering reputation for wise decisions and effective action, and the respect of country and party alike. When he took his seat, the Republicans controlled the Presidency and both houses of Congress; his friendship with the incoming Taft and the retiring Roosevelt was firm and unbroken. By each he was expected to be the bulwark of the new administration.

Actually, Root's six years in the Senate turned out to be the most unhappy and least successful part of his public service. His influence upon the nation's development between 1909 and 1915 was slight and of a negative sort. Moreover, when he voluntarily retired in 1915, his party was divided and out of power. The basic principles of government that he cherished were under attack, his health had been weakened, his integrity had been questioned, and the old relationship with Roosevelt shattered beyond repair. These indeed were the years of frustration.

The fundamental reason for these disappointments was that Root was out of tune with the times. He was an ingrained conservative in an age of progressivism. This age subjected to a searching re-examination accepted beliefs and standards in society, business, and politics and sought to restore to the people the control of their government that had been seized by the triumphant industrialists and financiers and their allies during the economic revolution following the Civil War.

Root was astonished, puzzled, irritated, and eventually overborne by this ferment of new ideas. For the moment his constructive work was suspended as he fought change and apotheosized doctrines of an age that was passing. Thwarted and saddened by the onrush of liberalism, he used his position in the Senate and as a leader of the American bar to extol the old order, and this defense of conservatism was his most important contribution to the Progressive Era.

These personal and political frustrations, however, lay beyond the horizon in November 1908. It was then that Root decided to exchange a seat in the cabinet for one in the Senate. In the preceding twelve months Roosevelt had regretfully but sagaciously chosen Taft, rather than Root, as his successor. Root never betrayed any disappointment at this fateful selection. Nor did Root nurse any resentment against the more available Taft. When the President-elect begged him to continue as Secretary of State, Root was sorely tempted. But his wife's wishes came first. She disliked Washington and wanted to spend a larger portion of the year in New York and Clinton. This could be more easily accomplished as Senator than as Secretary, and the dutiful Root acted accordingly. On January 19, 1909, the New York legislature elected Root to succeed Thomas C. Platt.

1. *The Coming of Progressivism*

There is no evidence that, prior to March 1909, Root was interested in or influenced by the writings that underlay progressivism. Even the beginnings of critical investigation into the framing of the Constitution and the working of the Supreme Court left him unimpressed. Unlike Roosevelt, he had few contacts with such reformers as Jane Addams, Jacob Riis, or Ray Stannard Baker. He had little love for the muckrakers; while Secretary of State, he had been pilloried by some of them for his record as a corporation attorney. In Washington he did not associate with the Middle Western progressives, soon to be known as the insurgents; and he had once referred to Hearst as "our New York La Follette."

Yet Root did not enter the Senate as an implacable foe of reform. He was not a reactionary. Under McKinley, he had been too absorbed in colonial and military problems to influence decisively purely domestic policy; but under Roosevelt, his advice was sought on almost every matter. Roosevelt asked the opinion of all his cabinet officers; but when the chips were down, he invariably turned, as he told Taft in August 1908 to turn, "to that ever present help in time of trouble, the beloved Root."

It is not easy, however, to generalize on Root's reaction to Roosevelt's progressive program. Although Roosevelt before 1909 was essentially a middle-of-the-roader, intent on maintaining the traditional order of society from the assaults of both capital and labor, he did dissolve or begin the dissolution of more trusts than historians have given him credit for; he did strengthen Federal regulation of railroads; and he did improve the lot of government employees. As his second term waned, he urged reforms that foreshadowed some of the ideas he was to advocate with more vigor and, perhaps, with more understanding when in 1912, after bolting the party, he stood at Armageddon and battled for the Lord.

If Secretary Root had misgivings over President Roosevelt's progressive tendencies, he kept them to himself. With his legal training and corporate experience he was undeniably more cautious than his chief, who had known neither law nor business. Yet in October 1906, Root enthusiastically endorsed a forthcoming Presidential message recommending an inheritance tax and further trust legislation. And there is no reliable evidence that he opposed Roosevelt's comprehensive program, set forth on January 31, 1908, of employers' liability, workmen's compensation, restricted use of the injunction in labor disputes, and additional Federal control of railroads, corporations, and securities. In fact, before 1909, Roosevelt always insisted that Root and Taft shared his views, and he frequently defended the former from the facile charge of having the outlook of a corporation lawyer. Root may not have had the crusading zeal of a Gifford Pinchot; but there was no reason to believe, when he entered the Senate, that he, any more than Taft, would soon diverge from Rooseveltian policies.

2. Conservatism Defended

Root's divergence after 1909 can best be understood by an analysis of his political thinking and by an examination of certain events during Taft's Presidency. Although widely hailed as the brainiest man in public life, Root never evolved a systematic philosophy of government. The only times he spelled out his ideas at length were in a series of four lectures at Yale in 1907 and in a pair of addresses at Princeton in 1913. But the former were devoted to underscoring the obvious, while the latter were confined to specific measures. It is significant that Root's most frequent utterances on government began in 1912, when his cherished but somewhat ill-explored beliefs were under attack.

If Root was not a profound political thinker, he did have strong convictions and the ability to express them clearly, forcefully, and in good temper. He started with an unshakable faith in the American constitutional system. He saw in its workings the fullest opportunity for the individual to develop his moral, political, and business qualities. There was nothing novel about Root's obeisance to individualism. His was a modified survival of nineteenth-century *laissez faire,* and it resembled the doctrine set forth a decade later by Herbert Hoover. Yet, as Morris Cohen has pointed out, Root combined this adoration of individual initiative and enterprise with a Calvinistic insistence upon the depravity of human nature, at least in its political manifestations.

Because man is errant, if not sinful, both singly and in mass, there must be, Root argued, certain restrictions upon his freedom of action. These restraints should be embodied in a written charter. They were, in Root's words, "rules of right conduct" that bound the citizen and his government alike. In his more impassioned moments the Senator asserted that these constitutional restraints represented "the eternal principles of justice." What he actually had in mind were the normal devices to protect the minority from the majority and the property of the individual from undue interference by the state.

As progressives questioned ever more closely the handiwork of the Founding Fathers and the machinery by which it was interpreted, Root grew more and more lyrical in his praise of the Constitution, more and more mystical in his references to the "eternal principles" upon which it was based. For once the hardheaded realist gave way to an emotional romanticist. There is no evidence that he read J. Allen Smith's *The Spirit of American Government*, published in 1907, or Charles A. Beard's *An Economic Interpretation of the Constitution*, which appeared in 1913. Root was not concerned with how the Constitution had been drawn up or even with the motives of the framers. Rather he was intent on maintaining it inviolate, and he deplored the frequent progressive demands to amend the charter of the national government.

In his construction of the Constitution, Root prided himself on being a staunch nationalist. John Marshall was his hero. But he was not oblivious to the threat posed to state sovereignty by the consolidating tendencies of modern industrialism. He often warned that each commonwealth must try to solve the social and economic problems within its borders lest the Federal government be compelled to act. Any state that shirked its responsibilities was, in effect, jeopardizing the freedom of its sisters.

There were two other points that Root reiterated endlessly in his vain battle to roll back the waves of progressivism. One was the virtue of representative government; the second, the need for an independent judiciary. Root distrusted the various proposals to make governmental machinery more directly responsive to the popular will. The American system, he maintained, was a representative one; and every scheme to curtail the authority of the legislature lowered the quality of those willing to hold office. As to the judiciary, Root doggedly fought plans to recall judges or their decisions by the voters. He believed that the courts alone could decide when the executive or legislative branch had exceeded its constitutional powers, and he regarded judicial review as the unique American contribution to the art of government.

If Root never formulated a comprehensive political theory, he was constantly forced to apply his ideas to concrete problems. He was willing to accept the direct primary for the nomination of state and national officials, if only because he was outraged by machine rule in New York. By 1915, at least, he was prepared to endorse the short ballot, workmen's compensation laws, and an executive budget system. But he objected to the initiative and referendum on the ground that they weakened the legislature. He conceded that some questions were simple enough to refer to the electorate, but most of them were not. The popular initiation of laws was even more hazardous. He was unalterably opposed to tampering with the state courts. To subject judges to an election immediately after handing down an unpopular decision would destroy their independence; to allow the people to pass upon complex judicial questions would entrust them with an authority they were ill-fitted to discharge.

At the national level, Root fought two of the three attempts to amend the Constitution. With some misgivings he acquiesced in the Sixteenth Amendment, which permitted a direct tax on personal incomes. He criticized, however, the Seventeenth Amendment on the familiar ground that the direct election of Senators would weaken the representative principle. He also doubted whether men of the highest caliber would be willing to serve in the upper chamber if they had to conduct periodically a state-wide campaign. As for the granting of suffrage to women, an amendment that did not pass during Root's term, he felt as strongly in 1915 as he had in the New York Constitutional Convention of 1894. Women, he declared, had no place in political life; to read his sincere but fatuous arguments one would conclude that to bestow the ballot on the fair sex would destroy American womanhood and break up the American home.

As a good Hamiltonian, Root was ready to accept certain progressive demands for increased governmental services and regulation. Under Taft, he backed the establishment of postal savings banks and the parcel post. He was not averse to expanding the jurisdiction of the Interstate Commerce Commission, but rather inconsistently drew the line at Wilson's Federal Trade Commission. As a matter of fact, the trust problem did not loom large in Root's writings.

Root was as quick to challenge attempts to change the national court system as he was with the state. On this point the Senator was often fighting phantoms, for very few progressives seriously considered applying the principle of recall to the Federal judiciary. Root insisted upon maintaining inviolate the process of judicial review, then under attack by some progressives, but was reluctant to eliminate obvious defects. He recognized that the Sugar Trust ruling in 1895 and the Lochner decision regarding hours of work for bakers in 1905 were mistakes, but he offered no solution to prevent similar errors in the future. Nor was he disturbed by the fact that five justices might interpret the "rules of right conduct" in one way, and four justices in another.

Root's emergence after 1909 as the defender of conservatism can be attributed also to his close relations with the Taft administration. Root and Taft had known each other since the early 1890's, had developed mutual respect during 1900–1904 when Taft ruled the Philippines under Root's direction, and had become fast friends after 1905 when they sat next to each other in Roosevelt's cabinet. Both reacted to the challenge of progressivism in the same way and for the same reasons. Both were affected by their legal training, their concern for an independent judiciary, their doubts about experiments in direct democracy, and their distrust of the Midwestern insurgents. As President, Taft leaned heavily on Root, and in 1911 appointed Root's disciple Stimson as Secretary of War.

In the days immediately after the election of 1908, Taft was less cautious than Roosevelt and Root. The major decision to be taken before the inauguration was whether to back "Uncle Joe" Cannon for another term as Speaker of the House of Representatives. Taft, who had learned on the stump how unpopular Cannon was, how widely he was regarded as the symbol of reaction, was eager to pass over the venerable legislator. Roosevelt, however, doubted the wisdom of taking such a gamble, and Root argued that the anti-Cannon forces in the House were still too weak to elect someone else. Taft was thus persuaded to support Cannon in 1909, and he eventually went much further than Roosevelt and Root envisaged. There is no evidence that Root approved Taft's subsequent alliance with Cannon, which so outraged the progressives; but he did like "Uncle Joe" personally and in 1913 did not hesitate to speak admiringly of the courage shown by the standpatter when he was under fire.

The opening legislative battle of the Taft administration came over the downward revision of the tariff. Root's contribution to the Payne-Aldrich Act was slight, but in a skirmish that formed part of the main conflict he found himself aligned against the progressives. The latter wished to offset the diminished revenue that would follow a tariff cut by a Federal tax on personal incomes, and in June 1909 they had enough votes to block any tariff bill unless some new impost on wealth was enacted.

Root opposed an income tax at this time. He believed that it should be levied only during national emergencies. In any case, he did not wish to embarrass the Supreme Court by subjecting it to popular pressure on a law it had declared invalid in 1895. As a compromise, therefore, Root suggested that Congress place an immediate tax on the income, not of individuals, but of corporations, and simultaneously send to the states for approval a constitutional amendment granting specific authority to the Federal government to impose a direct tax on personal incomes. Because of the delay involved in the second part of the plan, the progressives opposed Root's solution; but with the backing of the administration and of conservative Democrats it prevailed. As a result of this episode, Root came to be regarded as an exponent of Old Guard standpattism, not of Rooseveltian liberalism.

Much more distressing for Root was the Ballinger-Pinchot affair which rocked the administration to its foundations and widened the rift between Roosevelt and Taft. This *cause célèbre* grew out of charges made by Louis R. Glavis, Chief of the Field Division of the Interior Department, that his superior, Secretary Richard A. Ballinger, was permitting the government to be defrauded of valuable coal lands in Alaska. As President, Roosevelt had awakened the nation to the need for conserving its natural resources; and he had left behind a devoted band of disciples, headed by Gifford Pinchot, Chief of the United States Forest Service. Ballinger was scornful of Roosevelt's reliance on publicity; and when he ignored Glavis's accusations, the latter took his case to the President. Whether Ballinger was actually a foe of conservation or the victim of cruel injustice, whether Glavis was a zealous guardian of the nation's treasures or a reckless muckraker, and whether Pinchot subsequently helped or harmed the cause he had so much at heart are questions over which historians still disagree. For Root, the unhappy incident involved his loyalty to Taft, who was compelled to dismiss Pinchot; to Roosevelt, whose admiration for the chief forester was unbounded; to his protégé Stimson, who sided with his collegemate Pinchot; and to the party, whose unity was gravely threatened.

When Root was drawn into the imbroglio in mid-November 1909, most of the damage had been done. By then Taft had upheld Ballinger against Glavis and had entreated Pinchot not to make Glavis's cause his own. By then *Collier's Weekly* had leveled a muckraking assault upon the Interior Department and had retained Louis D. Brandeis to defend it in case a libel suit should result. By then Stimson had appealed to Root to persuade the President to re-examine the whole matter. Root replied he would do what he could, but he had little hope of averting a crisis that was "pregnant with immense evil for the Administration and the Republican Party."

In January 1910 the explosion occurred. Pinchot virtually dared Taft to remove him. The President turned to Root for counsel. After much soul-searching, the Senator advised dismissal, a step that was taken on January 6. Two weeks later Congress voted to investigate the Interior Department; and although Root preferred to stand aside, the administration refused to be deprived of his prestige, and he was named as one of five Senators on a joint committee.

From the outset, it was charged that Ballinger would be exonerated. Root deplored the widespread prejudgment of the case and the obvious intention of the progressives to use it to attack the President. Throughout the hearings, which lasted from late January to the end of May, he attempted to expedite the proceedings and to keep them within their original purpose. In so doing he repeatedly clashed with Brandeis. When the Boston attorney diverted his inquiries from Ballinger to Taft, Root snapped out that the Interior Department, not the White House, was under investigation. The Senator was probably a little overbearing and intolerant in his attitude, but he had some provocation for his impatience during the long and unhappy period.

On May 19, 1910, just before the final summing up, Root left Washington to argue an American arbitration before the Hague Court. He did not escape the troublesome case, however, as he ardently wished he might. Knute Nelson, chairman of the joint committee, sent letters to Europe and insisted that Root join his colleagues as soon as he returned. Nelson later credited Root with bringing order out of the committee's chaos, and there is no doubt that the final report of December 1910 owed much to Root's suggestions.

Root tried to keep that report moderate in tone and judicial in temper. He desired a restrained document, devoid of partisanship, that would contrast with the emotionalism of the muckrakers. He insisted upon the elimination of certain unfavorable reflections upon Pinchot and former Secretary of the Interior James R. Garfield, as well as upon the inclusion of several criticisms of Ballinger. But since the committee divided along party lines and since the Republican majority cleared Ballinger, Root's efforts were ignored by the public. To progressives, Root again appeared in the conservative camp and as somewhat less fair-minded than his reputation for integrity would have suggested.

Even before the Ballinger verdict was rendered, Root faced another unpleasant dilemma. Should he endorse the Taft administration in the mid-term election of 1910, an endorsement that Roosevelt, recently returned from Africa, was reluctant to bestow? Should he approve the "New Nationalism," the progressive program that the colonel expounded in the West during August and September? Should he send Stimson to almost certain defeat by urging his nomination for governor of New York? Root faced the election with deep pessimism. As early as February 11,

1910, he had written Roosevelt, "We have been in power for thirteen years and a good many people are getting tired of their rulers." In September he told Stimson: "The country has made up its mind to change parties. It is like a man in bed. He wants to roll over. He doesn't know why . . . but he just does; and he'll do it."

Root himself escaped the worst ravages of the Democratic resurgence in 1910. He managed to resolve his conflicting loyalties, for the time being, without antagonizing either Roosevelt or Taft. He helped the former to win his fight for temporary chairman in the New York convention, and together they wrote a platform that said nice things about the administration in Washington. Stimson was nominated and went cheerfully to his doom. In his main speech during the campaign, Root extolled Taft, Roosevelt, and Stimson. He insisted that the New Nationalism was an old Republican policy, and he praised judicial review as the palladium of liberty. He criticized, by implication, some of Roosevelt's recent remarks on the courts; but if the colonel caught the note, he remained silent.

For the party, however, November 1910 brought disaster. The Democrats wrested control of the House, and in the Senate the Republican margin was cut from seventeen to seven, thus giving the insurgents the balance of power. The retirement, death, or defeat of many party stalwarts left Root even more conspicuous among the defenders of conservatism.

The year 1911 was for Root the calm before the storm. He maintained his friendship with both Taft and Roosevelt, although with the latter contacts were becoming fewer and areas of disagreement more obvious. The Senator's opposition to progressivism was highlighted by his attack on the proposed Seventeenth Amendment and on the admission of Arizona to statehood with a constitution providing for the recall of judges. To be sure, he joined the progressives in a vain attempt to unseat William Lorimer, whose election had been palpably corrupt; but Root's vote was regarded as evidence of his devotion to political morality, not of his concern for political liberalism.

3. Conflict of Loyalties: 1912

In January 1912 an air of impending disaster hung over the once gay musketeers. D'Artagnan, restless at Oyster Bay, was consumed with disgust for his chosen successor and wracked by indecision over seeking the Republican nomination himself. Porthos sat in the White House, enveloped by gloom, alternately bewildered and angry, but constantly pursuing tactics least calculated to insure success and most designed to bring on the fight he did not want. In Haverhill, Aramis lay an incurable invalid, his brilliant judicial career prematurely ended. And in Washington, the normally serene and self-assured Athos, buffeted by a progressive storm he could not quell or, indeed, fully understand, for once failed to act with his customary decisiveness.

Why did Root hesitate in this moment of party and personal crisis? In 1920, after Roosevelt's death, Root told Taft that he had always blamed himself "for not taking hold of Theodore before the campaign of 1912 and making him see the lack of wisdom in the step which he took." Presumably, Root then believed that firmness on his part would have deterred Roosevelt from becoming a candidate. Contemporary evidence does not support such a conclusion; on the contrary, Root understood all too well how much Roosevelt had changed in the last two years.

Once Roosevelt sailed for Africa in March 1909, the old intimacy between the two men ceased. Relations continued cordial, and they exchanged occasional, affectionate greetings. Root amused the big-game hunter with such remarks as where Kermit had killed one lion with three bullets, his father had killed three lions with one bullet. They conferred together in London in May 1910, soon after Roosevelt emerged from the jungle and while Root was on his way to The Hague. Root explained the causes of the growing opposition to Taft and advised the colonel to be cautious. The latter, who had already seen the aggrieved Pinchot in Italy, apparently agreed but was unable to live up to his promise.

In September 1910, Root and Roosevelt fought side by side at the New York convention, but a divergent reaction to the progressive challenge pushed them in opposite directions. Root's identification with the Taft regime and his outspoken defense of conservatism disappointed the colonel, just as Roosevelt's new political associates and his attack on the courts alarmed the Senator. A trace of bitterness crept into a letter Roosevelt wrote to Root on October 21, 1910, in which he turned down a plea to campaign in Ohio for Taft. Three weeks later Roosevelt declared that although Root was the ablest man in public life, he was unfitted to grapple with the new conditions. And on January 2, 1911, the former President told Robert Bacon that he "greatly regretted" Root's having signed the joint committee report which censured Pinchot and Garfield.

Root sensed this change and put off, therefore, any heart-to-heart talk about Roosevelt's running in 1912. He was, moreover, embarrassed by the fact that he had committed himself to Taft's renomination before anyone thought Roosevelt might be a candidate. Hence it was not until the colonel, on January 26, 1912, sent him for comment a copy of a letter addressed ten days before to Frank Munsey that Root girded himself for the supreme effort. Even then there was an inexplicable delay of over a fortnight, during which time the Rough Rider moved steadily toward the decision Root was to advise against.

In his letter of February 12, Root ostensibly begged Roosevelt not to say anything that would encourage his nomination. In effect, he recommended that Roosevelt take himself out of the running completely. He rested his argument on the grounds of justice to Taft, the need for party unity, and the danger to Roosevelt's place in history. He was convinced that a Taft-Roosevelt fight in the convention would be so bitter that the Democrats would win in November by default. Root was too fond of Roosevelt to expose him to the charge of ingratitude or the risk of defeat.

Root's entreaties came too late. By February 12, the die had been cast. Two days before, seven Republican governors had invited Roosevelt, by prearrangement, to announce his candidacy; and the colonel had promised to reply within ten days. His answer to Root, the last exchange between the two men until 1918, was a friendly but firm refusal to stay out of the race.

Even if Root had not been already committed to Taft, he could not have followed his old chief in the campaign that followed. On February 21, in his Columbus speech, entitled "A Charter of Democracy," Roosevelt came out flatly for the popular recall of decisions of state courts. This and other attacks on the judiciary cost him the support in 1912 of not only Root but also other old and dear friends, such as Lodge, Stimson, George Meyer, and his own son-in-law, Nicholas Longworth. The lot of all these men was to be unhappy, but it was Root who suffered the most.

For it is one thing to refuse to follow. It is another actively to oppose. During the ensuing contest for the Republican nomination, Lodge chose the first course and Root the second. As a result, one friendship was kept up without difficulty; the other was ruptured beyond repair.

Late in May 1912, Root agreed to serve as temporary chairman of the Republican National Convention. Since it was evident that there would be a bitter battle to seat rival delegations, Root must have knowingly and deliberately placed himself in the direct line of Roosevelt's fire. Yet less than a fortnight before, when Roosevelt and Taft were trading savage blows and unseemly epithets, Root had refused to be drawn into the fracas and had bluntly informed the President that he could not campaign for him in critical Ohio.

The reasons given by Root at the time and afterward for this momentous decision are not completely satisfactory. He repeatedly declared that he had no right to refuse, that it was his duty to preside if asked, that someone must do the dirty job, and that it had fallen to him. It is unlikely, however, that he served against his wishes. It is probable that a passionate devotion to party, a profound conviction that unity was imperative, and a faint hope that he alone could insure, if not harmony, the triumph of sound conservative principles also influenced him. Whether he expected Roosevelt to oppose his selection is not clear. The colonel, although privately indignant at the choice, hesitated before announcing that Root was unacceptable to his forces. The Rooseveltians took the understandable position that if they held a majority of the delegates, they should also have a keynote address that accorded with their policies. Root the conservative could not be counted upon to sound the clarion call to progressives throughout the land.

Even before the discordant hosts of Republicanism assembled on June 18, 1912, Root was under a double progressive attack, first as the personal choice of Taft and secondly as the agent of the hated National Committee, which had for two weeks been deciding almost every disputed delegation in favor of the administration. Because of these rulings the Taft forces had a slight majority when the convention opened. They were able, therefore, on the first day to elect Root by a tally of 558–502. Since many of those voting for him had been put on the temporary roll over progressive protests, Root was at once charged with receiving stolen goods. The position to which he was elected, moreover, was not simply the temporary chairmanship, entrusted with the keynote address, but also the permanent chairmanship, which entailed presiding over the entire proceedings.

Late on the opening day, midst jeers and catcalls, Root began his keynote speech. Weakened by an attack of dysentery, he could hardly make his voice heard to the gathering which listened, for the most part, in stony silence. What he said was neither inspiring nor novel. He appealed for harmony, recited the achievements of the last three Republican administrations, and asserted that the Democrats were unfit to govern. The conclusion contained the message nearest to his heart, one addressed to the Rooseveltians and one they least wished to hear. Quoting from Hamilton, Marshall, and the platform of 1908, he restated his abiding faith in representative institutions, in a government clearly bound by constitutional restraints, and in an independent and untrammeled judiciary. Differently received in the rival camps, Root's words exerted no perceptible influence upon subsequent events.

The basic problem confronting Root as chairman in 1912 was the one that recurred in 1952. How should the claims of contesting delegates from the same state or district be resolved? The convention, of course, had the final word; but who in that body was entitled to vote? Could a delegate whose own seat was challenged but who had been placed on the temporary roll by the National Committee cast a ballot on disputed cases other than his own?

To Root the answer was clear and unquestionable. The rules of all previous Republican conventions, as well as those of the House of Representatives, decreed that no delegate could pass on his own right to be seated, but that everyone on the temporary roll was entitled to vote on all other contests. These regulations may have been unwise and unfair — the convention in 1952 decided that they were. They may have given the National Committee undue power and have stacked the cards in favor of the White House or its candidate. But they were the rules, and unless modified or repealed, the chairman must apply them.

Root's strict application of these rules in the convention insured the renomination of Taft. It was his action as chairman that infuriated Roosevelt and led to charges of theft and thwarting the popular will. How valid were these indictments?

That Roosevelt was the overwhelming choice of the rank and file of the Republicans is undeniable. That in the thirteen states utilizing the direct primary his vote exceeded that of Taft and La Follette combined is demonstrable. That the President's main strength came from the rotten boroughs of the South and the territories, which would provide no help in November, is likewise true. Roosevelt, moreover, symbolized a major liberal protest within the party against the old order and those leaders, like Root, who resisted the progressive impulse. Yet of the 254 disputed delegates, the convention awarded only nineteen to the Rooseveltians. Historians agree that the colonel was entitled to another twenty-five or thirty, that over one hundred of his cases were spurious, and that the rest involved questions over which, as Root said at the time, honest men might disagree. Had the progressive faction received its due, it could have prevented the selection of Root, but it could not have forced the nomination of Roosevelt.

Root's handling of the turbulent convention was masterly. Grimly determined, he was swayed by neither truculent delegates nor the incessant "toot-toots" from the gallery, intended to signify displeasure at the steam-roller tactics of the majority. At times speakers could not be heard. One began with a classical, "Gentlemen, lend me your ears." Waiting in vain for silence, he quickly substituted the more plebeian, "Boys, give me a chance." Only once did a flicker of a smile pass across the chairman's countenance. A Southerner rose to a point of order. When asked to state it, he declared, "The point of order is that the steam roller is exceeding the speed limit." Midst gales of laughter Root replied: "The chair is ready to rule upon the point of order. The point of order is sustained. The justification is that we have some hope of getting home for Sunday."

No incident in his life brought greater sorrow to Root than the Chicago convention. When the Roosevelt forces walked out of the hall and thus made certain the nomination of Taft, the breach of friendship was complete. Root's integrity was assailed. The colonel said many harsh things about "the thieves of Chicago," and occasionally in public linked Root with the most reactionary and corrupt elements in the party. Root never replied in kind. He refused to engage in personal recrimination, a lifelong practice which, in this case, was fostered by continuing affection for an old friend.

For Root was convinced his course had been correct. Like Jim Bludso, the creation of the beloved Hay:

> He had seen his duty, a dead-sure thing —
> And he went for it thar and then.

Root believed he had saved the party and the principles which had made it great. He agreed with Taft that the outcome of the convention was more important than that of the election. The conservatives retained control of the party machinery; and even if Taft lost in November, a loss Root anticipated, a conservative would be chosen in 1916. Actually, Root's estimate was correct only because Roosevelt had bolted. If he had remained in the convention, he or a follower would, after a Taft defeat in 1912, almost certainly be nominated four years later, to the great benefit of progressivism in general and to the liberal spirit in the Republican party in particular.

Root was certain not only that he had acted wisely but also that a clash between the two wings of the party had been unavoidable. Writing on July 8 to the disconsolate Robert Bacon, he said: "Disease not checked in time reaches a point where there is absolutely nothing to be done . . . The process that has begun must go on. No human power can prevent it. . . . I personally have much regret, but I am saved the pain of doubt, for I have not for an instant the slightest question as to what my course ought to be and must be."

Having exposed himself fully to the Rooseveltian wrath, Root, somewhat quixotically, took almost no part in the ensuing campaign. On August 1, while Congress was still in session, he did have to make a short speech, in his capacity as chairman of the convention, formally notifying Taft of his nomination. In this he agreed, after urging by the President, to put his personal stamp on the Chicago proceedings. "Your title to the nomination," he asserted at the ceremony, "is as clear and unimpeachable as the title of any candidate of any party since political conventions began." But with that chore behind him, Root resisted all of Taft's frantic appeals to take the stump; and Lodge, who had escaped the colonel's ire by remaining at home during June, was drafted on one occasion to take Root's place. That Root suffered a nervous reaction after the convention and that he was stricken with grippe in October cannot be denied, but it is equally evident that he had no stomach for a canvass that offered more opportunity for personal abuse than for party victory. In the end, he confined himself to one major speech.

Taft's crushing defeat in November was accepted by Root with equanimity. Politically, the task ahead was clear. The Republican party must be revitalized on a sound conservative basis, free from progressive heresies. Personally, the outlook was less certain. Root knew Roosevelt too well to expect that complete reconciliation, even if possible, would be easy or prompt. For the time being, passions must be allowed to subside in the hope that some common cause or objective might later draw the old friends together again.

4. *Frustration: The New Freedom*

If the conflict of loyalties in 1912 led to political disaster and personal sorrow, the aftermath was a period of frustration. The last two years of Root's Senate term were Wilson's first two in the White House, and they found the New Yorker in a novel role. For the only time in his public career he belonged to the minority. For the only time he was not, as it were, a power behind the throne. After March 4, 1913, the doors at 1600 Pennsylvania Avenue rarely opened to him. The occupant was a comparative stranger; and the relations between the two men, at first polite and cordial, steadily deteriorated. Most of the cabinet was unknown to Root, and the new Congressional leaders were, in many cases, persons he had previously regarded as incompetent. Inevitably Root's attitude toward his duties changed. With less power to shape legislation and with less sympathy for what was being attempted, he gradually became obstructive rather than constructive.

Under these circumstances, Root's achievements as Senator were meager. He opposed almost every item in Wilson's domestic program. This opposition was at first temperate and courteous. It was free from the pettiness and vindictiveness that marked the attitude of Roosevelt and Lodge. By 1915, however, Root had begun to lose his tolerance and fairness; eventually he came to hate Wilson as he had never before hated a man in public life.

The first business on Wilson's agenda was tariff revision. On September 9, 1913, the Underwood-Simmons bill passed the Senate by 44–37. Root voted nay. Although a protectionist, he objected mostly to the section on the income tax. On April 21, 1913, he told Mrs. Hay that the men "who are planning the Income Tax don't care a hang about charities . . . What these people want to do is to take away the money of the rich, classifying as rich all who have over four thousand dollars a year, and then to pass laws distributing it among their people at home."

The second of Wilson's major objectives was reform of banking and the currency. In a long speech on December 13, 1913, Root spoke out strongly against the Federal Reserve Act. He professed to be sympathetic to the broad purposes of the plan, but attacked its details as a spur to inflation. His address, based on material supplied by New York bankers, attracted considerable attention; and it may have resulted in one significant amendment. But this concession did not satisfy Root, and he voted in the minority when the bill passed six days later by 54–34.

The same negativism appeared in Root's reaction to other Wilsonian legislation. He regarded the proposed Federal Trade Commission as inquisitorial and would have voted against its establishment if he had not been playing hookey in Clinton during August and September of 1914. He disliked certain features of the Clayton Anti-Trust bill but, apparently, not strongly enough to stay in Washington to protest. He was absent on September 2, 1914, when the act was first passed; and he cast a negative ballot on October 5, when it came back from conference. Root was also against the La Follette Seamen's Act of March 4, 1915, which, in its later stages, was more a progressive than a Democratic undertaking.

The extent to which Root was at war with the New Freedom was clearly revealed in his address at the Republican State Convention in Saratoga on August 18, 1914. He contended that the new tariff had hurt industry without reducing the cost of living, that the Federal Reserve Act had frightened capital from embarking upon new ventures, that the income tax had discriminated against the Eastern states, and that the Federal Trade Commission was another dangerous step toward government by administrative bodies. Root's severest indictment was that the New Freedom was based upon jealousy and hatred of the successful businessman.

If the last two years of Root's term in the Senate were thwarted ones, he suffered another disappointment in 1915, one that can barely be mentioned. That was his labor as president of the New York Constitutional Convention which sat at Albany from April to August. Partly out of a sense of civic duty and partly to obtain the incorporation of sound conservative principles in the new state charter, Root agreed to repeat his services of 1894. Two decades before, he had been Choate's first lieutenant; now his was the guiding hand and the dominating voice. He received effective support from two Republican associates, Stimson and George W. Wickersham, and from a new Democratic friend, Alfred E. Smith. Under Stimson's promptings,

Root went further than ever before to try to reconcile his ideas with moderate progressive principles. The whole nation watched the proceedings; knowing politicians whispered that a successful outcome would stamp Root as the logical Republican candidate for the Presidency in 1916.

Root had not been bitten by the Presidential bee, but he was eager to win approval for the new organic law. To his intense disappointment, as well as to the amazement of those outside the state, the voters in November 1915 rejected the new constitution. This defeat was additional evidence that the Progressive Era brought to Root, not the unbroken series of triumphs he had won as Secretary of War and of State, but rather a sense of frustration that made him yearn to return to private life.

As early as September 22, 1911, Root had expressed his intention not to run again for the Senate. It is likely that he would have retired even if there had been no intraparty struggle, but the events of 1912 confirmed his resolution. In May 1912 he wrote that he would "declare my independence of all constituencies . . . except Mrs. Root, and . . . devote myself to amassing a fortune on the farm at Clinton, with just enough incidental intellectual occupation . . . to ward off softening of the brain." Not even the importunities of friends like Stimson could change his mind; on June 29, 1914, he informed party officials he would not seek re-election.

The reasons for this decision were simple. With Mrs. Root in indifferent health for some time and with his own doctor warning against the rigors of another six years, Root was glad to yield to a younger man. At seventy he felt entitled to leisure. The break with Roosevelt, the party schism, and the frustration of being a minority Senator had removed all the pleasure and satisfaction of political life. Under the Seventeenth Amendment, Root would have to be re-elected by popular vote; but although he did not relish the idea of a state-wide campaign, Root did not quit because he was afraid of it.

It is interesting to speculate whether Root might have reconsidered if he had foreseen the outbreak of the European war. His last efforts in office had been directed toward defeating the Wilson administration on the Ship Purchase bill, the first Congressional battle over neutrality. This struggle ended on March 3, 1915; and three days later, in a farewell note to Justice Holmes, Root said: "There is something rather somber about this climbing up on the bank and looking back at the stream . . . Curiously enough, the bully big fight we have just had in the Senate makes me sorrier to go than I thought when there was nothing doing except a lot of scrapping over little things in which I took no interest." Whether the Federal Reserve System and the Clayton Anti-Trust Act were "little things" may be doubted; but there is an appealing note to this au revoir from a seventy-year-old Senator to a seventy-four-year-old Justice, especially when the latter had twenty more years to live and the former, twenty-two.

The one positive aspect of Root's work in the Senate can be found in diplomatic problems. As a former Secretary of State, he was placed at once on the Committee on Foreign Relations. There, until March 4, 1913, his influence equalled that of the active Lodge and exceeded that of the indolent chairman, Shelby M. Cullom. Even after the Democrats took over, Root was treated with deference by the new chairmen, Augustus O. Bacon and William J. Stone. Wilson and Secretary Bryan, until August 1914 at least, frequently sought his advice, as Taft and Knox had done before them. He figured prominently in Senatorial struggles over arbitration, Mexico, the Panama Tolls Act, and the disposition of German ships interned after August 1914.

Unlike his terms as Secretary of War and Secretary of

State, Root's service as Senator was devoid of any long-lasting achievements. In foreign affairs his influence was considerable but not decisive at any one place. In the domestic sphere no important law is associated with his name, and the course of legislation would not have been very different if he had never sat. The reason for this unexpected absence of constructive work, for this rather appalling waste of talent, is that he was out of sympathy with the prevailing trends of the day. The true significance of these six years in his life, so far as internal problems are concerned, is not his role as a lawmaker but his attempt to define and defend the conservative tradition in an age of progressivism.

V

The First World War:

Belated Interventionist 1914-1918

DURING THE FIRST WORLD WAR, Elihu Root was primarily an observer and a bystander. Although he became a prominent critic of Wilson's neutrality and ultimately an interventionist — belatedly, to be sure, but still before the President — he was not in a position to influence the most fateful decisions. Nevertheless, he was frequently in the public eye. No study of this critical period can ignore Root, even though his role was markedly less than both Wilson's and Roosevelt's.

If Root's was not the decisive voice during American neutrality and belligerency, the First World War did form a significant chapter in his life. It aroused deep emotion and constantly occupied his mind. It filled a vacuum created by his withdrawal from the Senate, kept his name before the people, and insured a continuing interest in public affairs that was to extend beyond the armistice and cause him to play a notable part in the peacemaking. It would be a mistake to minimize the importance of these years to him just because his accomplishments were less tangible than those of his cabinet service.

Root's deeds and words after 1914 have meaning for the historian as well as for the biographer. Most writings on America's road to war in 1917 have been so centered

upon the struggle between Wilson and the nonintervention-
tionists that they have tended to obscure a third position,
whose exponents believed the President's resort to arms
was too slow rather than too fast. Certain historians in the
1930's were so convinced that American participation was
needless and unwise that they ignored, or dismissed scorn-
fully, those who maintained that it was necessary and desirable. Even today there is a relative neglect of those who
insisted that the United States had a greater stake in Europe's battle than Bryan's followers would concede and
who demanded a bolder policy toward Germany than the
Wilson administration would adopt.

The Republican chieftains who had guided American
foreign policy before 1913 — Roosevelt, Taft, Root, and
Lodge — stood at the forefront of this group, ably seconded
by former Secretary of State Robert Bacon, former Secretary of War Henry L. Stimson, former Ambassador Joseph H. Choate, and former Chief of Staff Leonard Wood.
All were ready, well before the President, to enter the
war; but although they agreed generally among themselves on the ideological and strategic reasons for that step,
because of individual temperament or position held, they
differed in the timing, manner, and method. Root felt as
strongly on the issue involved as anyone of this group; but
he chose to keep silent until February 1916 and, even after
that date, tried to conceal beneath a calm, judicious de-
meanor the constant agitation and mounting impatience
he experienced as the war progressed. Publicly, he was a
moderate and belated interventionist, for he did not
openly advocate American belligerency until after diplomatic relations with Germany were severed early in February 1917.

In considering Root's role in the events leading to America's entry into the First World War, it is necessary to establish at the outset his place on the national scene. After

March 4, 1915, he was, for the first time in a decade, a private citizen, though hardly an ordinary one. An acknowledged expert on diplomatic and military problems, he shared with Taft the leadership of the conservative wing of the Republican party, and there were some who regarded him as a logical standard-bearer a year hence. As president of the Carnegie Endowment for International Peace, of the American Society of International Law, and of the American Bar Association, he was strategically situated to mold public opinion. His failure to wield a power commensurate with his opportunities can be attributed partly to his preoccupation until November 1915 with the proposed New York constitution, partly to a temperamental reluctance to assail Wilson on foreign policy until it was absolutely necessary, partly to an advancing age which sapped his strength and his ambition, but mostly to an unwillingness and inability to be a tribune of the people, as Roosevelt always was, or their educator, as Taft became.

1. Background to War

Root's attitude toward the First World War was the product partly of past events and earlier beliefs and partly of his reaction to developments as the conflict proceeded. Before 1899, Root seldom referred publicly or privately to international affairs. His was, however, no provincial outlook; he had traveled abroad widely and frequently. Like many of his contemporaries, he reacted strongly to certain episodes during the war with Spain, especially those involving Germany and England. As early as 1900 he expressed fear of German penetration in the Caribbean.

As Secretary of State, Root had no real trouble with Germany, but he always feared the worst. He revealed his uneasiness in his handling of the conferences at Algeciras and The Hague. He resented Germany's refusal to conclude an innocuous arbitration treaty in 1908, the only major power save Russia to hold aloof. His relations with England, on the other hand, offered a sharp contrast. With Ambassador Bryce he established an intimacy that carried beyond 1914; and he was able not only to settle the hoary North Atlantic fisheries controversy but also to liquidate several troublesome disputes with Canada. In short, his cabinet experience made Root more kindly disposed toward Britain than toward Germany, just as he traced his revered principles of constitutional liberty to Westminster rather than to Berlin.

During the Taft administration, Senator Root had little opportunity to deal with matters that became prominent during the World War; and even under Wilson his handling of foreign affairs down to August 1914 is significant mainly for the light it throws upon his relations with the President. At first, Root and Wilson saw eye to eye on several external issues. The most important was the need to repeal the exemption clause of the Panama Tolls Act of August 1912. Root had objected strenuously when Taft had approved a bill exempting American coastal shipping from tolls to be levied when the Panama Canal was completed. He believed that such discrimination violated the Hay-Pauncefote Treaty of 1901, a belief shared by Choate, Lodge, and Henry White, all of whom had been connected with the negotiation of that pact. Taft and Knox reasoned differently; and when they rejected a British protest, Root assumed that the dispute, involving the interpretation of a treaty, would be arbitrated under his own bilateral agreement of 1908. To his consternation, Taft and Knox, who had been so ardent for a broader arbitration pact in 1911, refused in 1912 to resort to the existing one.

Disgusted by hypocrisy in his own party, Root launched a drive in January 1913 to repeal the exemption clause. At the same time he helped to persuade President-elect Wilson to advocate the same policy. The ensuing struggle was difficult and unpleasant. Those championing repeal were denounced as Anglophiles and tools of the transcontinental railroads, while news that the Carnegie Endowment for International Peace had spent money to disseminate information on the subject was used to embarrass Root. Nor could Wilson carry out his promise to push the measure until he had got part of his domestic program through Congress. Not until June 1914 was the repeal bill voted by the Senate and approved by the President.

There were other areas of agreement between Root and Wilson. Both wished to renew the arbitration treaties which Root had negotiated in 1908 and which were to expire in 1913. The Senator's silence on the administration's steps during the Japanese crisis, precipitated by the California Land Law, appeared to denote acquiescence. Nor did he oppose Bryan's conciliation or "cooling off" conventions, though he stated privately that they were of very limited utility. Neither Root nor Wilson wished to interfere in the Mexican civil war; and in August 1913, when the President's policy was being attacked by Lodge and other Republicans, Root gave out an interview in which he completely approved of Wilson's hands-off tactics. This timely endorsement, which might not have been forthcoming if Root had not been out of the country for a month, drew from the White House a warm note of thanks.

This honeymoon between Root and Wilson on foreign affairs could not last, and it ended before the lamps went out all over Europe. Quite apart from a divergence on domestic issues and the disdain Root felt for Bryan as Secretary of State, they eventually found themselves disagreeing on several points. Root disliked the original draft of the Bryan-Chamorro Treaty, which would have created a protectorate of sweeping proportions over Nicaragua. He was dismayed by talk of early independence for the Philippines and by the acts of the new governor general, which upset the pattern established by Root and Taft a decade earlier. He was infuriated by a proposed settlement with Colombia that expressed regret for what had happened in 1903 and promised a large monetary compensation. Root considered this solution inferior to his own of 1909 and also a gratuitous insult to Roosevelt.

Even on Mexico, the Senator began to criticize the President. He questioned the wisdom of repealing the arms embargo in February 1914, for the move was clearly designed to aid the Carranza faction. In April, he and Lodge led an assault on an administration-drafted resolution empowering the executive to act during the Tampico crisis. Root felt that any intervention should be based on the injuries done to American citizens and their property, not on an ideological or personal desire to oust President Huerta. By summer he was censuring Wilson for doing the very thing he had promised not to do, for taking sides in the civil war. Root's contempt for what he considered the President's blundering in Mexico soon knew no bounds.

In short, by August 1914, Wilson's domestic and foreign policies had drained almost all of Root's reservoir of good will, and there was every reason to expect the Senator to examine most critically the President's handling of the European war.

2. *Taking a Position*

The outbreak of hostilities caught Root, as it did all his countrymen, by surprise. Just because they were so unprepared for the onset of Armageddon, many Americans made statements in August 1914 that they later wished had been left unsaid or, conversely, were silent when they subsequently regretted that they had not spoken out. The failure to protest against the invasion of Belgium or to demand some action by the Hague signatories was to embarrass men like Root and Roosevelt when they later castigated Wilson for not having put the United States on record as disapproving on moral grounds of the various initial German moves.

It is easy to understand why Root was silent in the first weeks of war. During the deceptive lull between the murder at Sarajevo and the ultimatum to Serbia, he had fled Washington to escape both the heat and the futility of combating Wilson's domestic program. He had planned to sail for Europe on August 22. At Clinton he was cut off from the latest news, as well as from the opportunity to voice his opinions on the Senate floor. He was tired, irritated and physically below par. Such energy as he could muster was devoted to keeping conservative the Republican party in the state.

Under these circumstances, Root found it convenient to adhere to his practice not to speak for publication. Like all Americans, he felt it a patriotic duty not to embarrass the President, a feeling shared in August and September even by Roosevelt. Wilson's appeal of August 18 for impartiality in thought as well as in action made it inappropriate for a member of the Committee on Foreign Relations to rush into print. Premature criticism was also estopped by the fact that several of Root's friends were helping to formulate policy. Robert Lansing, whom Root had backed for the post, was counselor of the State Department, Chandler P. Anderson was a legal adviser, and James B. Scott was chairman of the State, War and Navy Joint Neutrality Board.

Root's silence on the issues of the war did not denote doubt or indifference. With a rapidity and a certainty that belied his reputed judicial manner of thinking, he reached by August 5 basic conclusions from which he never budged. The Kaiser, he wrote, was determined to dominate Europe. For years he had dreamed of conquest, and his decision to strike in 1914 had been taken even before the ultimatum was handed to Serbia. For the moment, Root thought, the United States could do nothing. The Hague machinery was inadequate. The neutrals could help most when hostilities had ended.

The recurrent theme of Root's letters during the fall of 1914 was that the American people had reached a "swift and positive judgment" on the causes and meaning of the war. They were outraged by the callous invasion of Belgium, by the brutal destruction of Louvain, and by the cynical references to a scrap of paper. The Allied case he deemed unassailable. It needed no argument or propaganda. The facts spoke for themselves. England and France were "fighting for the causes of liberty and peace and humanity." He hoped that ignorance of the legitimate rights of belligerents to restrict certain types of neutral trade would not blind American public opinion to the true facts of the case. To dispel such ignorance, Root persuaded the State Department to brief newsmen on the rudiments of international law and thus prevent the inevitable disagreements between the United States and the Allies from reaching the headlines.

Root's simple analysis of the origins and nature of the First World War alienated, when it became known, the German-Americans and the Anglophobes. The next generation, disillusioned by the apparent futility of the Great Crusade, came to regard him as a warmonger and a dupe. Even his official biographer, writing in 1938, was out of sympathy with Root on this point. Undoubtedly there was an element of superficiality in Root's thinking; but today, after a second global conflict, one is less likely to criticize his conclusions than the manner in which he reached them. In 1914 he was unusually dogmatic and cocksure, even though the facts, which supposedly spoke for themselves, were taken, so far as the diplomatic background was concerned, solely from British sources.

During his final session in the Senate from December 1914 to March 1915, Root said little on the general issues of the war. He was, however, confronted with one concrete problem affecting American neutrality and on it he took a firm stand. That was the Ship Purchase bill.

The outbreak of hostilities had posed a very real problem for American farmers by reducing drastically the amount of shipping available to move crops to Europe. Debts had already been incurred in anticipation of this seasonal trade; and if the exports were choked off, many Southerners and Westerners faced ruin. To secure additional tonnage, Congress passed the Ship Registry Act, which enabled American citizens to purchase foreign-built vessels without the restrictions previously in force and permitted German nationals to transfer their ships to a dummy concern under a United States registry. Although some legislators warned that the Allies would not respect the American flag on merchantmen bought from the Central Powers, the bill became law on August 18. Both Root and Lodge were absent, the former vacationing in Clinton, the latter stranded in London.

This first move did not please everyone, least of all the Secretary of the Treasury. Fearing that private capital would be insufficient to obtain a large number of vessels, McAdoo proposed that a government-owned corporation be created with authority not only to purchase ships but also to construct them. It was this plan, still pending when Congress met in December 1914, that aroused and angered Root.

Root's opposition to the Ship Purchase bill was fourfold. First, he feared international repercussions. He was positive, and here both Bryan and the Joint Neutrality Board agreed, that to buy belligerent vessels in this manner was unneutral. He was certain that the Allies would not permit German ships, heretofore interned in American ports, to carry precious war materials to the continent under the Stars and Stripes. Even if the sale did not incite Allied reprisals, it would complicate an already dangerous controversy over neutral rights.

In the second place, Root regarded the measure as a thinly disguised scheme to help Germany. German ships tied up in American harbors constituted the major tonnage for purchase, and the Reich would be enabled to convert a huge liability into a handsome profit. Thirdly, Root resented the steam-roller tactics employed by the majority to jam the bill through Congress. Boasting that they had the votes and that debate was futile, the Democratic leaders held day and night sessions in order to wear down the Republican Senators, many of whom, like Root and Lodge, were over sixty-five. Lastly, the plan would put the government into competition with private enterprise. Normally, Root would have inveighed against such a socialistic scheme, but in 1915 the first three arguments were uppermost in his mind.

The Senate battle lasted through January and February. Root made three speeches on the subject, something most unusual for him. One dealt with the attempt to curb full discussion, one with the precedents of international law, and one with the economic implications. A filibuster ensued, during which Root reached the limits of physical exhaustion. In the end, his side triumphed, and the administration received its first major setback. Although the bill passed the House on February 15, no vote was reached in the Senate.

Root's fight on the Ship Purchase bill was an exception rather than the rule. He said little about Germany's alleged atrocities, except that he did not think the Carnegie Endowment for International Peace was the proper agency to investigate the truth of the charges. He did not comment on the initial ban on loans to belligerents, on Wilson's "strict accountability" note to Germany on February 10, 1915, or on Japan's conquest of the German colonies in the Pacific and her presentation to China of the Twenty-one Demands. He approved of Bryan's refusal to prohibit the exportation of arms and munitions, arguing that the rules of neutrality must not be changed in the middle of the game and that free trade in armaments was the only safeguard for peaceful nations against militaristic neighbors. Although he did not join in the opening drive for preparedness in 1914, he did urge the Democratic spokesmen in Congress to appropriate $200,000,000, which Wilson might employ on the armed forces at his discretion; but this suggestion, reminiscent of the sum given McKinley in March 1898, was never acted upon. Before March 1915, Root did not in any way recommend that the United States enter the war or take steps that would lead inevitably to intervention. For him there was a clear distinction between desiring an Allied victory and taking up arms to insure one.

3. *The Road to War*

For eleven months after quitting the Senate, Root maintained his silence on the problems of the war. For much of the time he was occupied with the New York constitution; and although he followed American diplomacy avidly, his comments are to be found only in the letters and diaries of his friends. He adamantly refused to be quoted by the press as crisis succeeded crisis.

Not until February 15, 1916, did Root emerge as a major critic of Wilson's foreign policy. The occasion was an unofficial state convention at Carnegie Hall, and Root was selected to deliver the keynote address. His acceptance of this assignment can be attributed to several factors. For some time he had craved to speak his mind. He had tolerated what he regarded as Wilson's blunders long enough. He was particularly aroused when the President, for tactical reasons, declined to make a fight in Congress for Secretary of War Garrison's plans to enlarge the army. He was disgusted by the appointment on January 31, 1916, of Louis D. Brandeis to the Supreme Court; and in a move that he apparently never afterward regretted, he joined with Choate, Taft, and other past presidents of the American Bar Association in a memorial to the Senate Judiciary Committee alleging that Brandeis was unfit to be on the highest tribunal in the land.

Political considerations also entered into Root's willingness to address the state gathering. His friends were insisting that he be a candidate for the Presidency; and while he never deluded himself on that matter, he was eager to use the opportunity to commit his party to a strong stand on foreign affairs. It is possible that Root knew about Secretary of State Lansing's proposal of January 18, 1916, to abandon an earlier position and henceforth prohibit armed belligerent merchantmen from entering American ports. This plan would hurt the Allies, but it might persuade Germany to operate her submarines according to traditional rules of cruiser warfare. At any rate, Root was certainly aware of the mounting Congressional demand to keep Americans off such belligerent ships, a demand that would soon explode in a dramatic challenge to Wilsonian leadership. But even if he had been oblivious to these matters, Root would have said what he did.

He began with a sharp attack on Wilson's Mexican policy. The President, he charged, had failed to protect American lives and property; he had interfered foolishly and futilely in the civil war; and he had gained the enmity of both sides. Root then condemned the unpardonable delay in launching a preparedness program, one that would strengthen American diplomacy and protect the nation in the perilous days ahead. He also blamed Wilson for not protesting against the invasion of Belgium and for not summoning the Hague signatories to take steps to uphold the agreements of 1907, but this criticism was most unfair inasmuch as neither Root nor Roosevelt had themselves urged such a move in August 1914.

The heaviest blows, however, he reserved for Wilson's repeated threats and subsequent failures to carry them out. The President, Root asserted, had made a mockery of his promise to hold Germany to "strict accountability." His "too proud to fight" speech had cost the United States the respect of all virile peoples. America, it seemed, could be defied with impunity. "No man," he warned, "should draw a pistol who dares not shoot. The government that shakes its fist first and its finger afterwards falls into contempt."

As a partisan arraignment of Wilsonian leadership,

Root's address was a huge success. Not bothered by the need of formulating a positive program, not concerned with the perplexing day-to-day problems, Root ruthlessly exposed the policy of drift which had rendered America, as Walter Lippmann had put it seven weeks before, uneasy and distraught. Lodge was delighted by the performance. Taft considered the tone too Rooseveltian and guessed that its wholesale denunciation would weaken Root as a possible candidate. Four months later, after the conventions, Roosevelt called it a "really great speech," one that marked the beginning of a proper Republican stand on preparedness. Even the *New Republic*, a frequent supporter of Wilson and a past critic of Root, declared that "the speech . . . may well be the forerunner of a new epoch in American foreign policy." Root, it said, had expressed forcefully the malaise which had crept over sensitive Americans and had revealed how public opinion could be molded by real leadership.

In subsequent issues, the *New Republic* qualified this lavish initial praise. It quickly noted the apathy, even hostility, to Root's ideas among Midwestern Republicans. It quite properly accused him of second-guessing on the Belgian and Hague issues and of glossing over such immediate problems as the armed ship controversy. Lodge asserted that Root's speech, together with efforts by himself and Senator Sterling, had been instrumental in causing Lansing to abandon his plan to placate Germany on that point; but Root never claimed as much. He was satisfied with a more limited effect. "You have no idea," he wrote on February 18, "what a relief it is for me to have spoken out at last. . . . I hope that the Party will stand up to it."

One consequence of Root's address, somewhat exaggerated in importance at the time and since, was his first meeting with Roosevelt in five years. The persistence of strained relations between the two men saddened mutual friends, all the more so since Roosevelt was again on intimate terms with others who had left him in 1912. Hoping that a common outlook on the war might provide a basis for reconciliation, Robert Bacon arranged a luncheon at his home on March 31, 1916. Only Bacon, Root, Roosevelt, Lodge, and Leonard Wood were present. The past and future of the Republican party were discreetly ignored, since Roosevelt was ostensibly still a Progressive. The conversation centered upon the need for preparedness and the perversity of Wilson.

Coming only two months before the Republican and Progressive conventions, this so-called "harmony luncheon" touched off a wave of speculation and rumor. Some newsmen asserted that Roosevelt would support Root for the Presidency; others declared that Root had lured a willing Bull Mooser back into the folds of orthodoxy. Actually, because of these political overtones, the meeting produced little concord.

The chasm that still separated Root from Roosevelt was strikingly revealed in the political conventions in June 1916. The former had reluctantly, perhaps amusedly, permitted his admirers to launch a Presidential boom. Headquarters were opened in several cities, and on April 7, seventy prominent New Yorkers publicly endorsed Root. Simultaneously, the colonel at Oyster Bay was wracked by the same indecision as four years before. Could he capture the Republican nomination? Should he keep the Progressives as a separate entity? In this fluid situation one thing was certain. Although both men desired a reunited Republican party as the best means of ousting the despised Wilson, Root was dead set against the selection of any bolter of 1912, and Roosevelt would not tolerate anyone connected with the so-called "steal" of that year. Neither, in short, would support the other.

The Root boom never got going. The beneficiary refused to lift a finger in his own behalf and was content to tie up a number of delegates, mostly from New York, whom he might later throw to some conservative. During the spring many groups did "roost with Root," as the saying went, but he had no possibility of winning unless Supreme Court Justice Charles E. Hughes declined to run or unless Roosevelt persuaded the Progressives to back his former Secretary of State. Perhaps both developments were necessary; neither came to pass.

So far as Root was concerned, the critical moment in the Republican convention occurred in the early morning hours of June 10, 1916. Two ballots had been taken and the next would come when the gathering reassembled before noon. Hughes, who had let it be known that he would accept the nomination, was far out in front with 328½ votes to Root's 98½. Roosevelt trailed badly; but if he acted before the third roll call, he might still secure for another what he could not obtain for himself. By long-distance telephone he was asked to endorse Root as a means of stopping Hughes, a man the colonel disliked. Without an instant's hesitation, Roosevelt said flatly he could not discuss Root's candidacy. Although he wanted to see Root back in the State Department, he could not forget 1912. He suggested the equally conservative Lodge and Wood as compromise possibilities for both conventions; but neither man was acceptable. The result was the nomination of Hughes on the third ballot by the Republicans and the early demise of the Progressives as a national party.

Root was not disappointed or resentful. Because of his record as a corporation attorney, he never regarded himself as a Presidential candidate. Moreover, it is doubtful whether, even with Roosevelt's backing, Root would have been nominated by the Republicans in 1916. Nor is it likely, as Nicholas Murray Butler always contended, that Root could have beaten Wilson and thus changed the course of history. Root might have avoided some of Hughes's mistakes, and he would not have wobbled so badly on the war issues. But the demand for a bolder policy toward the Central Powers would have not only alienated the German-Americans but also run into a rising antiwar sentiment. On domestic issues, Root would have attracted even fewer independents and progressives than Hughes did.

In the campaign itself, Root played a very minor part. Neither his hatred of Wilson nor the prospect of being Secretary of State if Hughes won could lure him on to the stump. He did help bring Roosevelt and Taft together at a reception in New York on October 3; but it is significant that for this first public meeting of the two men since the bitter days of 1912, Root undertook to secure Taft's acceptance, not Roosevelt's. On October 5, Root made his single major speech in Carnegie Hall. He again indicted Wilson's blundering in Mexico, his procrastination on preparedness, and his irresolution in holding Germany to "strict accountability." He gave the President no credit for having kept the country out of war, and he strongly criticized various domestic measures. Although the *New Republic* called it "clearly the ablest and most destructive argument put forth by any Republican in the campaign," Root offered only a cogent partisan arraignment, not a constructive program.

When California's long-delayed returns disclosed that Wilson would serve another term, Root was plunged into deep gloom. Never before in his adult life had the Republicans been out of office for eight consecutive years. More immediately, German diplomacy seemed to be outmaneuvering the Allies, and he feared that both the administration and the people were turning against the Entente Powers. He was sickened by the deportation of Belgian laborers and blamed Germany for this at a mass meeting on December 15, 1916. Then came the publication of Wilson's request that all belligerents state their war aims. Rather unfairly, Root interpreted the President's statement as a blunt assertion that both sides were fighting for the same ends and that no greater moral issue was involved than in a dogfight. Already Root had privately branded Wilson as unscrupulous and dishonest; now he called him incredibly blind.

Indignant as he was over Wilson's tergiversations, Root still could not bring himself to assail the President as Roosevelt was doing. Hence, in speaking before the National Security League on January 25, 1917, he referred to the "noble idealism" in Wilson's "Peace without Victory" address three days earlier, a concession that infuriated Lodge and Roosevelt. Stimson assured the latter that Root had intended to be ironical; but if that were so, almost all the newspapers missed the point. In the rest of his speech, however, Root did dissent from the President's position. A peace without victory, he warned, was not enough if it was not the right kind of a peace. Autocracy must be destroyed and the Allied objectives must be achieved, even if it meant a war of conquest.

Despite his mounting condemnation of Wilson's policies, Root never once before the break with Germany advocated outright American participation in the war. He did not urge such a step publicly or privately. Nor did he demand a line of action that would inevitably lead to entering the fray. Root was an interventionist, but a belated one. Unlike Roosevelt or the ardent American Rights Committee, who would have broken off diplomatic relations after the sinking of the *Lusitania* in the confidence that hostilities would quickly ensue, the cautious Root did not recommend war until the withdrawal of the *Sussex* pledge seemed to leave no honorable alternative.

After the rupture of diplomatic relations on February 3,

1917, Root was eager to enter the fight. He shared none of Wilson's faint hope that Germany might yet spare American ships, and he went through none of Wilson's mental agony in sending America's youth to the blood-soaked Western front. Yet unlike Roosevelt, he gave the President a reasonable time to hasten preparations. Outwardly he spoke of "standing by the President"; in private conversations he was not so tolerant. He grew steadily more impatient. He chafed at the delay in enlarging the army, opposed the idea of a war of limited liability — in which the United States would simply repel attacks upon itself — and insisted upon an all-out effort in close co-ordination with the Allies.

The final statement of Root's position came in speeches before the Union League Club on March 20 and at Madison Square Garden on March 22. Germany, he asserted, was already at war with the United States, destroying lives and property. If the nation did not defend itself now, greater indignities would follow. At the close of hostilities it would face a German challenge in the Western Hemisphere that would transform the United States into an armed camp and could, conceivably, demolish the Monroe Doctrine. The Allied cause was the cause of the American people; self-respect required that all Americans now do their part.

In analyzing Root's justification for intervention, one is struck by his silence on many of the reasons stressed by historians of the interwar period. He gave no weight to the pressure exerted by bankers, munitions makers, or Entente propagandists. He ignored the changed character of twentieth-century warfare, a change that invalidated or made a mockery of established rules of international law. He did not attribute American involvement to the diplomatic ineptitude or pro-Allied bias of its leaders. He regarded the ultimate German menace to American institutions as very real. On the other hand, unlike certain writers of the 1940's, he never spoke of the need for preserving Anglo-American control of the Atlantic. There is no evidence that he believed Germany was winning the war or that she would triumph unless America intervened. He was not interested in fighting to create a league of nations. What he did say was that the United States was being attacked, that self-respect and self-interest demanded it meet the challenge, and that failure to do so would spell danger and disaster for the future.

Wilson's eloquent war message to Congress on April 2, 1917, received Root's heartiest approval. Like Lodge, he momentarily forgot the old Wilson and declared that the President had nobly expressed the true sentiments of the American people. A personal note of congratulations to the White House was acknowledged as "very gracious and generous." Root told Lansing that it was a "bully address," and on April 9, he urged the Republican Club of New York to back the President 100 per cent. He asked that partisan obstructionism be eschewed, contended that a coalition cabinet was not necessary, and insisted upon a vigorous prosecution of the war. To gain the last end speedily, he recommended a universal military service law, an expeditionary force to France at the earliest possible moment, and a suspension of premature discussion of peace terms.

4. *The Mission to Russia*

Root's most important contribution to the conduct of the war came soon after the United States entered the conflict. In May 1917 he headed a mission to Russia, designed to demonstrate American good will toward the Provisional Government and to discover what was needed to prevent that strife-torn nation from making a separate peace.

The reasons for sending a group of prominent Americans to Petrograd, then, were obvious. The United States had been the first to extend recognition after the revolution of March 12, 1917, and it was imperative to capitalize on Russian gratitude by strengthening the government of Prince Lvov against the radical Bolshevists, who would repudiate all past obligations and come to terms with the Kaiser. The triumph of Lenin would free Germany to fight a one-front war.

The reasons for selecting Root to head the delegation were more complex and more questionable. Secretary of the Treasury McAdoo and Secretary of State Lansing wanted Root, partly because they respected his diplomatic talents and partly because his appointment would underline the administration's nonpartisan approach to war problems. Perhaps Root's generous appeal of April 9 to uphold the President reassured Wilson of his loyal co-operation. Both Lansing and Edward M. House, Wilson's intimate adviser, had called attention to that speech. By April 19, the President agreed to name Root provided Lansing found, on conversation, that he was "a real friend of the revolution."

Since, presumably, Root did not wish to restore the Romanovs, he was offered the job and on April 24 accepted it. It was no slight task for a man past seventy-two to embark upon a rigorous journey through a land seething with unrest, one that might at any time fall to the invader or explode in revolution. Root was not eager to go, but he felt he had no choice. He had advocated war; now he must do his part, just as those who volunteered or were drafted did theirs. He must demonstrate the willingness of Republicans to co-operate with the President.

Whether he believed he could accomplish very much the records do not divulge.

The announcement of Root's appointment, even the rumor of it, unleashed a torrent of criticism. Wilson was told that the job was not one for a blind reactionary or for one who had consistently opposed his domestic program. The radical socialists proclaimed that Root would be a *persona non grata* to the revolutionary workers, while Jewish organizations charged he had, while Secretary of State, truckled to Russia. The President was apparently not prepared for these attacks; and although he stuck by his choice, he probably regretted it even before Root departed.

In a brief life of Elihu Root there is no space to describe in detail his dramatic visit to Russia. Nothing he did or did not do affected the outcome. It is enough to say that his group left Washington on May 15, 1917, crossed the Pacific on an aged navy cruiser, traversed Siberia in the Tsar's special train, spent four weeks in Petrograd with occasional side trips, and returned by the same route, reaching the capital on August 8. Save for extending greetings to the existing government, delivering innumerable addresses that were soon forgotten, and collecting information that was soon outdated, the mission accomplished little of value. "It was," Root said in 1930, "a grand-stand play." Some historians, however, believe that the mission was prevented by economic and class prejudices from advising a realistic policy.

The real significance of the episode is the influence it had upon the subsequent relations between Root and Wilson. The latter came to regard the mission as a fiasco. In his opinion, Root had failed utterly to win over those elements in Russia that distrusted the Allies. He had painted a ridiculously optimistic picture of the stability of the Provisional Government, and he had not foreseen the

Bolshevist uprising of November 1917. Wilson later felt Root should never have been sent. As Raymond Robins, head of the American Red Cross group, subsequently wrote to Roosevelt, "Root in revolutionary Russia was as welcome as the smallpox, and occasioned as much enthusiasm as would be aroused by an Orangeman leading a popular parade in Dublin."

In justice to Root, it must be said that all the commissioners — and they ran the gamut of political and social beliefs — were too optimistic in their analysis of conditions, at least in the parts released to the public. Wilson, moreover, had only himself to blame for the selection; but in this case, as in others, he ignored his own responsibility for appointments he afterwards regretted. However that may be, the President believed, rightly or wrongly, that Root had been tried and had been found wanting. He was to remember this experience and the criticism it had exposed him to when he came to choose the delegates to the Paris Peace Conference.

For Root, too, the Russian mission bequeathed bitter memories. He had grievances of his own. The most important was the reception, or lack of it, accorded to his major recommendation. While in Petrograd, he and his associates advised that a broad publicity campaign be launched at once to inform the Russians of the Allied war effort and to counteract the peace propaganda of the Germans. On June 17, 1917, they requested authority to draw $100,000 immediately; ultimately they might need up to $5,000,000. Whatever the price, the commissioners argued, it was a cheap one to pay for keeping Russia in the war. To their dismay, two weeks passed without a reply. On July 2, they sent a second cable, renewing the request and stating that Root and two other delegates had advanced $30,000 from their own pockets to begin the work. Not until after they had left Petrograd was the expenditure of this $30,000 approved. As for the rest, the State Department needed time for further study. That was the last Root heard of the plan he had sponsored.

There were other sources of annoyance. Root had no voice in the selection of the commissioners and their assistants. He was saddled with colleagues not of his choosing. Despite an invitation from Japan, the mission was not allowed to visit Tokyo on its way home. Lansing and, apparently, Wilson feared Root might express his views rather than the administration's. Most galling of all, however, was the attitude the delegates encountered upon their return. A few brief audiences at the White House and the State Department, polite but unresponsive readings of the voluminous reports, were followed by silence and inaction. In later months, when the Russian problem was very much to the fore, the advice of Root and his colleagues was never sought. This cavalier treatment of a distinguished statesman, whose diplomatic experience antedated that of the chief executive, infuriated Root and his friends. It confirmed Root's belief that Wilson was selfish and opinionated and that no self-respecting man with an independent mind could work successfully with the President. Nor was this slight forgotten when Root examined Wilson's own performance in the Treaty of Versailles.

For the rest of the war, Root held no other government post, but he followed events closely. For him, as for many Americans, the conflict became a crusade to extirpate autocracy and militarism. Despite his veneration for the law, Root was prepared to accept a temporary suspension of civil liberties. "You cannot," he declared on September 3, 1917, "have free democracy and successful war at the same moment." Although before his friends he privately flayed Wilson, he publicly urged a moratorium on all needless criticism of the government. He pointed out that mistakes were inevitable in wartime and that partisan or personal sniping at the President and Congress only weakened popular confidence in the nation's leaders. As might be expected, Root regarded all opponents of the war as pro-Germans, Bolshevists or "Parlor Socialists of the New Republic stripe." He had no sympathy for, indeed he never understood, dissenters like Robert M. La Follette or Randolph Bourne. He even went so far as to favor the elimination of German instruction in public schools lest it retard the use of English.

As the war lengthened, Root grew more dogmatic on its causes and its meaning. The keen, logical brain, noted for its ability to strip issues of all false connotation and sentiment, yielded to a religious, an almost mystical interpretation of the European cataclysm. The struggle, he asserted on March 7, 1918, was not one to annex territory or to redress wrongs done to Belgium and others, or to repel attacks on American citizens and shipping. It was, rather, to maintain "all the progress that the civilization of a century has made toward Christianity. . . . It was a war between Odin and Christ." And who willed American participation? Not the President, not the Congress, not the press, not any individual or group. It was nothing less than "the mighty forces that determine the destinies of mankind beyond the control of human purpose" which compelled Americans to take up arms in order "that the world shall be free."

In America's war effort, Root, of course, ranked far below Wilson. By the very nature of his office, the President is the dominant figure in any national crisis. During the conflict Wilson's voice did dominate; and his speeches set a standard in eloquence and vision which Root could not, or did not, match. Among the Republicans, Roosevelt, Taft, and perhaps Lodge, probably molded more minds than did Root.

Like many conservatives, especially those interested in foreign affairs, Root was alarmed by the First World War. German aggression, as he sincerely believed it to be, endangered a stable and orderly world, while German military tactics made a mockery of international law and the arbitral process on which he had long relied. It would be a mistake, however, to assume that only conservatives reacted as Root did to the Kaiser's bid for continental hegemony. Liberals like Herbert Croly, Walter Lippmann and even Wilson were equally fearful. Nor should one conclude that Root advocated American intervention to preserve the existing balance of power. Although concern for the established order was prominent in his thinking, he refused to demand outright participation until his country, in his opinion, had been attacked. At that point, he entered the conflict without fear and without regret.

V I

The Treaty of Versailles:

Constructive Critic   1918-1920

ALTHOUGH PREJUDICE AND PROVINCIALISM combined with personal and partisan rivalries to imperil the Treaty of Versailles in 1919, there were many Americans who opposed the pact, as drafted, for additional reasons. These citizens believed that the Covenant of the League of Nations constituted too sharp a break with tradition. The aim of these fair-minded, constructive critics — of which Root was one — was not to destroy Wilson's ambitious scheme, but rather to modify it so that it would conform more closely to what the American people had accepted in the past and to what they might reasonably be expected to undertake in the future. These critics believed the President had gone too far, too fast, and that a compromise between his idealism and their realism would better serve the national interest.

In his approach to the peacemaking, Root, as a true conservative, tried to reconcile the old and the new. His concern for America's role in world affairs antedated that of Wilson. He readily understood the stake his country had in the struggle that began in 1914 and in its ultimate settlement. But when Wilson, commencing in 1916, challenged his countrymen to push beyond the limits of their past experience, Root hesitated. He argued instead for keeping within more familiar confines and for building more systematically upon what had gone before.

Between Root and Wilson there existed an honest difference of opinion and emphasis that transcended mutual antipathies and conflicting party loyalties. The one, sensitive to precedent, stayed within the American tradition; the other, his eyes on the future, proceeded with a liberal's impatience to reach his goal. Responding to a conservative's faith in the judicial process, Root sought order and stability through the formulation and application of international law. Wilson, the innovator, on the other hand, thought in terms of a quasi-legislative body with broad authority. Root, with the example of the two Hague conferences in mind, was content to hold periodic gatherings of the nations and to rely on arbitration and conciliation. Wilson, however, insisted upon a more permanent organization, complete with council, assembly, secretariat, and judiciary, one that could draw upon military might to compel obedience and to defend the territorial integrity of every member state. On the question of using armed force to preserve peace, the two men were irreconcilable.

That Root also heartily disliked Wilson by 1919 is undeniable. He had accumulated over the years a long list of grievances that robbed him of all tolerance and forgiveness. Bitter memories of the New Freedom, of a hesitant neutrality policy, of the thankless Russian mission, and, as he thought, of a half-hearted prosecution of the war crowded in upon him as he watched the President blunder in his October appeal for a Democratic Congress, pass over every prominent Republican in selecting the peace delegation, and then sail away to Paris without even a gesture in the direction of consulting or conciliating a hostile Senate. Wilson's antipathy against Root was equally marked. During the negotiations he made no real effort to seek Root's advice and virtually ignored the recommendations Root sent to Paris.

Nor can it be denied that Root's approach to the peacemaking was affected by a deep loyalty to the Republican party and an unshakable friendship with Henry Cabot Lodge. After eight years in the political wilderness, eight years that witnessed unprecedented social and economic legislation, Root yearned for a return to normalcy. He would not wreck a peace treaty simply to insure a party triumph in 1920, but he certainly would not permit its details to bring about another disastrous schism. The lesson of 1912 was always before him as he searched for a program upon which most, if not all, Republicans could unite.

As to Lodge, it is enough to say that Root never failed to respond to appeals for help, and they were many, from the Massachusetts Senator. The two men did not always see eye to eye, certainly not after March 1920; but Root consistently gave his friend the benefit of the doubt, assuming that the person on the spot knew the situation best. The conclusion is inescapable that Root would have acted differently during 1918–1920 if Lodge had died when Roosevelt did.

To this day, historians still wonder whether Lodge desired, as he professed, a league of nations in some shape or form. Root's position has also puzzled scholars. By many he has been regarded as a friend of the treaty, one who would have been satisfied with minor changes and who honestly strove for its ratification. By others, he has been considered a calculating and dangerous opponent, one who subordinated principle to partisanship and who concealed his obstructionism under a cloak of ostensible fair play.

The problem in respect to both men is complex. With the situation constantly changing from February 1919 to

November 1920, they had to shift their views to meet the specific issue before them. It is customary to categorize those who approved the Versailles Treaty as drafted as nonreservationists, those who opposed the Covenant in any form as irreconcilables, and those who would accept the League of Nations with changes of varying severity as mild and strong reservationists. This division, however, applies only to the period between June and September 1919. Before June, the issue was one of amendments or rejection, not of reservations. After September, there were few who honestly believed that the original treaty could pass the Senate, and the real question was one of what reservations must be appended.

At the outset, Root contended as Wilson did that the United States must join with certain other countries to prevent future wars, but he parted company in wishing to separate the details of any such league from the peace treaty itself. After the Paris Conference had decided against him on that point, Root accepted the fact; but he did insist upon amendments to the Covenant that was completed on February 14, 1919. When the Covenant was revised and presented again on April 28, Root was still dissatisfied. He did not, however, demand further amendments but was content to accept the document with such reservations as would express the Senate's understanding of certain ambiguous clauses and would free the country from undesirable obligations in others. This policy of consent with reservations was Root's major contribution to the treaty fight, and he never deviated from it.

In short, Root was tolerant of but never enthusiastic over the original Treaty of Versailles. Despite his hatred of Wilson, he would have accepted the League of Nations, though with significant but not crippling changes. For most of the period he can be grouped with the mild reservationists; but because of his indignation at the President's tactics and intransigence and because of his desire for party unity, he often worked closely with the bitterest Republican opponents of the Covenant. Until March 1920, the difference between him and Lodge was one of degree, not of kind. After that date the two men drew steadily apart in their positions, though not in their friendship, as the Senator from Massachusetts abandoned the ranks of the strong reservationists and joined the irreconcilables.

1. *Prewar and Wartime Planning for Peace*

Like most Americans before 1914, Root optimistically believed that war was a relic of the past and that the steady development of international law and the broader use of arbitration could relieve tensions between states. Yet he recognized that there were practical limits to the arbitral process, and in two instances between 1909 and 1918 he clearly foreshadowed the stand he was to take on the League of Nations.

The first concerned the arbitration treaties that Taft and Secretary of State Knox negotiated on August 3, 1911. These were designed to enlarge the classes of disputes to be handled by that procedure, and they confronted Root with a difficult choice. Although its intentions were excellent and its objective laudable, the administration failed badly in its execution and submitted an agreement that was certain to antagonize the Senate and to dismay realistic observers of the international scene. But because the end was desirable, many educators, clergymen, and pacifists overlooked the details and blindly supported the treaties, declaring, in effect, that they provided a clear test of whether one favored doing something for world peace. Such loose thinking disgusted Root, as he was to be dis-

gusted when similar arguments were offered in behalf of
the Covenant of the League of Nations.

Root's dilemma was doubly difficult. Although he regarded the finished product of Taft and Knox as unsatis-
factory, he hesitated to join the opposition. As author of
the arbitration agreements to be replaced, he would expose himself to a charge of not wishing to improve upon his
own labors. As a former Secretary of State, he was reluctant
to encourage the growing practice of the Senate to amend
or defeat treaties. Moreover, the chief sponsors of the pacts
were his close friends, Taft and Bryce, and his protégé
Chandler Anderson. He had even been consulted during
the negotiations, although not on one objectionable provision inserted at the last minute.

On the other hand, there were good reasons to withhold
his consent. Roosevelt and Lodge were bitterly hostile to
the move, and in the summer and fall of 1911 Root was
eager to check the deepening estrangement between Taft
and Roosevelt. Even more important was his conviction
that the treaty committed the American people to a policy
they would not live up to when the crisis came. In 1911
Root used the same argument that he would apply to the
Covenant in 1919: to accept sweeping obligations that
might not be respected in the future was a hindrance, not
a help, to world peace.

Faced with a Hobson's choice, Root in August 1911
sought the path of compromise. On the one hand, he refused to endorse the treaties without some change. On the
other, he declined to vote for outright amendments, as
Roosevelt, Lodge, and many Senators wished. Instead, he
proposed to include in the resolution of ratification an
interpretation or construction of one controversial clause
and eliminate, thereby, several sources of danger.

In the end, Root's tactics failed. Although Knox for the
administration and Lodge for the Foreign Relations Com-

mittee eventually acquiesced in Root's method, they could not command two thirds of the Senate. In March 1912 that body deleted part of the text and included in the resolution of ratification such drastic reservations that the entire purpose of the treaty was vitiated. Root voted against these changes, but they passed and Taft was compelled to abandon his entire plan.

Root's reaction to the Wilsonian settlement could also have been foreseen by his attitude toward the League to Enforce Peace, the most important wartime agency for mobilizing American sentiment in favor of participation in a postwar organization. Founded on June 17, 1915, this unofficial body elected Taft president and numbered among its most active members A. Lawrence Lowell, head of Harvard University. It proposed that, at the close of hostilities, the United States join "a league of great nations," which would require each member to submit all justiciable questions, not settled by diplomacy, to a judicial tribunal, to refer nonjusticiable questions to a Council of Conciliation, to employ force jointly against any signatory which went to war without first resorting to the foregoing procedures, and to encourage the holding of periodic conferences whose major purpose would be the codification of international law.

To this specific and comprehensive blueprint for world peace there were divergent reactions. Wilson withheld his endorsement until May 1916 and then annoyed Taft by injecting the league idea into his peace negotiations with Germany. This tendency to identify a league of nations with a "Peace without Victory" outraged Lodge and prompted him in January 1917 to withdraw the support he had given eight months before. Roosevelt was openly hostile until August 1918, when his reconciliation with Taft enabled him to confer a very qualified approval.

The severest handicap suffered by the League to Enforce Peace was the abstention of Root. Little was expected
from the bellicose Roosevelt or the politically sensitive
Lodge. But Root's world-wide reputation as a devotee of
international law made him eagerly sought after. One of
the first acts of the executive committee was to invite
Root to become a vice-president and a member of that
board. On several occasions in 1915 and 1916 both Taft
and Lowell pleaded with him, but in vain. Root would
not join.

The reasons for Root's refusal are significant. He readily conceded that the League to Enforce Peace was a valuable instrument for educating the public. He highly approved of the planks calling for a wider use of arbitration,
a Council of Conciliation, and the periodic conferences to
codify international law. He vigorously opposed, however,
the obligation to use military force against any member
that violated its pledges, a far-reaching innovation that
Wilson accepted, apparently without hesitation. Such a
commitment, Root said, was an entangling alliance of the
worst sort and could never command the support of the
American people. In his criticism of the League to Enforce
Peace in 1915–1916, as in his objections to the Taft arbitration treaties in 1911 and to the Wilson Covenant in
1919, Root was consistent. He would make no promise that
was likely to be repudiated in the future.

2. Drafting the Treaty

Among the many difficult decisions Wilson had to make
in his quest for a just and lasting peace, none was more
far-reaching than his determination to attend the Peace
Conference himself and the choice of the other delegates.

Contemporaries and historians have debated the wisdom of his own participation and the appropriateness of his associates. On the first point, opinion is divided, though Root always held that the President should have stayed at home. On the second, there is little disposition to criticize Secretary of State Lansing, Edward M. House, or Major General Tasker H. Bliss, especially since the last was a belated selection in place of Secretary of War Newton D. Baker, whose presence in Washington was required after the resignation of Secretary of the Treasury McAdoo. Most students feel, however, that Wilson, if restricted to a single Republican, could have done better than Henry White. White was an accomplished career diplomat and an intimate friend of Root, Roosevelt, and Lodge; but he utterly lacked standing in the party or influence in the Senate. Whether the naming in late November 1918 of Taft, Root, Hughes, or Lodge (Roosevelt had but six weeks to live) could have overcome the innumerable obstacles Wilson faced — many of them of his own making — is impossible to say; but there can be no doubt that Root's attitude toward the Versailles Treaty would have been different if he had been one of the framers.

There was some reason to suppose that Root might be appointed a peace commissioner. Of all Republicans, he was best equipped to deal with foreign statesmen. His prestige as former Secretary of State, as judge on the Hague Court, and as recipient of the Nobel Prize, his success in charming Latin America in 1906, and his ingenuity in drafting a world court plan in 1907, all stamped him as an obvious choice. Unlike Taft, Hughes, and Lodge, he had not publicly attacked the President for the ill-fated October appeal to the voters, so that, whatever his true feelings about Wilson may have been, he seemed to most people less of a partisan than the other Republican chieftains.

Despite newspaper rumors and the expectations of Root's friends, Wilson never seriously considered taking him to Paris. To be sure, Root was recommended strongly by House and by Joseph P. Tumulty, the President's secretary, and moderately by McAdoo and Lansing. But Wilson's first choice was Justice William R. Day, a veteran of the treaty of 1898, and after him, White. Even former Governor Samuel W. McCall of Massachusetts and an obscure Minnesota Congressman had a better chance than Root. Wilson's reasons were expressed clearly when he wrote McAdoo on November 25, 1918, that Root was "a hopeless reactionary" whose appointment "would discourage every liberal element in the world." At other times he was quoted as saying that labor would not approve, that Europe regarded Root as an advocate of dollar diplomacy, that distrust of his conservatism had accounted for his failure in Russia, and that he was not in sympathy with the President's peace plans.

Save for the last reason, which was only partly correct, Wilson's explanations are unconvincing. In negotiating a postwar settlement and charting a course for the future, it is desirable to enlist the best brains of the country and not quibble over a man's views on domestic issues. There was nothing reactionary in Root's analysis of the world situation. He and Wilson certainly did not agree on every point, and Root was less ambitious and optimistic regarding a league of nations. But the idealistic President, inexperienced in the give and take of diplomacy, would have benefited at Paris from Root's realism and healthy skepticism, as well as from the esteem in which he was held in government circles in England and France. As for Root's potential influence in winning over the Senate, Wilson, to his sorrow, forgot that entirely.

Actually, Wilson's motives were simple if not commendable. He was temperamentally unable to work closely with men of stature, and he avoided coadjutors he could not dominate. Root would have been too strong an associate, no matter what his beliefs were. It is obvious, moreover, that each man disliked the other and that in his hour of triumph the President lost all sense of fairness toward political opponents. At this time he was equally contemptuous of the mild-mannered Taft upon whom he was later to rely heavily in his campaign to sell the League of Nations to the people.

Although the evidence is slender and, in some cases, negative in character, it is possible to reconstruct Root's views during the early stages of the Peace Conference. Like most Americans, he said very little about those sections of the treaty that did not deal with the League of Nations. He did not object to Japan's retention as mandates of the German colonies across the American line of communications to the Philippines, while he appraised realistically rather than emotionally the unpopular Shantung settlement. Though he was to draw back before certain sweeping commitments in the League Covenant, he was perfectly prepared to modify traditional isolationism by signing a defensive alliance with France.

As to a league of nations, Root had sent his ideas to Colonel House for Wilson long before the specific plan emerged from the conference rooms in Paris. Root recognized, he wrote in August 1918, the need for some machinery by which those nations concerned with a breach of peace could act. He preferred a loose entente to a tightly integrated league, and he objected to any automatic obligation to go to war without Congressional sanction in each specific case. He was convinced the people were not yet ready for any such pledge. What they would approve, because of past experience, was the Hague Conference method of developing international law, the establishment of a permanent court to handle all justiciable disputes, and a council of conciliation to make recommendations in non-justiciable controversies.

On February 14, 1919, the Paris Conference approved the Covenant of the League of Nations, and Wilson, after being out of the country for over ten weeks, headed home. During his absence, Root had kept silent on the peace-making. Although we know from later statements that he considered Wilson's failure to consult the Senate in December a shocking example of bad taste and worse tactics, he had not joined in the Republican sniping that followed the President's departure. In these weeks Root apparently had no correspondence with Lodge and no part in the strategy that led on March 3, 1919, to the "round robin," a warning issued by more than one third of the new Senate that the Covenant, as drafted, was unacceptable and should be separated completely from the formal peace treaty.

At this time, Root's opinion of the Covenant was not publicly known. Upon landing in America, Wilson laid plans for a nonpartisan mass meeting to be held at the Metropolitan Opera House in New York the evening before he returned to Europe. His advisers were eager to enlist the support of Root and Taft, either as speakers or committee members. On February 25, Tumulty inquired of Taft, then stumping the country, how Root stood on the Covenant. Taft had to confess his ignorance, but undertook the delicate task of persuading his old friend to share the platform with Wilson and himself. From Atlanta he wired on February 27, 1919:

IF YOU THINK YOU CAN SUPPORT CONFIRMATION OF PARIS COVENANT, AFTER AMENDMENTS THAT SHALL NOT DESTROY ITS SUBSTANCE, I THINK IT IS YOUR DUTY TO JOIN ME IN SPEAKING WITH THE PRESIDENT . . . I HAVE WORD FROM THE WHITE HOUSE THAT THEY ARE ANXIOUS TO SECURE YOUR SUPPORT.

From New York on February 28, where Root had already declined to serve as chairman on arrangements, came a laconic reply worthy of Calvin Coolidge:

THANKS, I THINK I WILL NOT SPEAK.

Root never explained why he would not appear with Wilson and Taft on March 4, but the reasons can easily be inferred. First of all, he was shocked by the President's cavalier refusal to call the Senate into special session to deliberate upon the Covenant. Secondly, he found that document to be a badly written mixture of good and evil, desperately in need of revision. Finally, reading Wilson's mind more expertly than Taft did, Root feared that the chief executive might take advantage of his presence to announce a policy he could not endorse. That, in effect, is what happened. On March 4, Wilson defied the Republican ultimatum implicit in the "round robin" and promised that, far from separating the Covenant from the treaty, he would bring them back so intertwined that they could not be parted without destroying both. Even Taft was dismayed by that unexpected and unwise bravado.

In the fortnight after Wilson sailed back to Paris, there arose a widespread demand that the Covenant be amended. Into this discussion Root was finally drawn. On March 9, 1919, White cabled Lodge to discover what amendments would satisfy the Senate. Fearing a trap, Lodge appealed for advice to Senator Frank B. Brandegee of Connecticut, an irreconcilable, who in turn sent Chandler Anderson to consult Root. Root was likewise suspicious and told Lodge to reply that no one could speak for all the Republican Senators and that if Wilson desired to know their wishes, he should call the chamber into special session. Lodge followed Root's recommendation to the letter, and for the next eight months he turned constantly to him for counsel.

As a private citizen, Root felt able to do what Lodge, as

the new chairman of the Foreign Relations Committee, could not. When he learned that his suggestions might be welcome in Paris, Root formulated on March 26, 1919, six amendments to the Covenant. These sought, among other things, to give greater prominence to the use of arbitration, to provide for the regular codification of international law, to insure a revision of the Covenant after five years, and to place the Monroe Doctrine and certain domestic policies beyond the authority of the League. Most important of all, Root advised that the obligation under Article X, soon to be the storm center of the treaty fight, be limited to five years. This Article, as adopted on February 14, 1919, stated:

The High Contracting Parties undertake to respect and preserve as against external aggression the territorial integrity and existing political independence of all States members of the League. In case of any such aggression, or in case of any threat or danger of such aggression, the Executive Council shall advise upon the means by which this obligation shall be fulfilled.

Before Root could discover whether his thoughts would bear fruit at Paris — and for the most part they did not — he agreed to make his first public statement on the Covenant. Lodge, Stimson, and Will H. Hays, the able and energetic chairman of the Republican National Committee, had all asked him to chart the course for the party to follow. Root's answer was contained in a prearranged letter to Hays, dated March 29, 1919, and published two days later. It attracted wide and favorable notice and seemed to command the support of even such isolationists as Senator William E. Borah, a leading irreconcilable, and George Harvey, a gifted though venomous journalist, soon to be one of Warren G. Harding's closest advisers.

Root began by assuming that all Americans desired some sort of postwar international organization. The charter just drafted possessed, he said, many excellent provisions; but some changes were indispensable. He then listed his six amendments, noted above, marshaled arguments in their behalf, and recommended that, if they were incorporated in the final draft, the Covenant be approved.

April 1919 was a month of watchful waiting as Wilson toiled manfully to secure some of the many changes requested of him. This was the crisis of the conference, with bitter quarreling over French security, naval limitations, reparations, Shantung, and Fiume. There can be no doubt that Root and others, not on the spot, grossly underestimated, then and later, the enormity of Wilson's task.

On April 28, 1919, the revised Covenant was adopted, and the Republicans had to decide whether the improvements were sufficient to warrant an endorsement of the entire document. The decision was not an easy one; for the party was divided, in and out of Congress, at the very time that unity was essential for organizing the new Senate. With the division standing at forty-nine Republicans and forty-seven Democrats, the slightest defection would be disastrous.

At this critical juncture Lodge besieged Root for advice with two long-distance calls and a lengthy letter within twenty-four hours. He also dispatched, for consultation with Root, Brandegee, and George W. Pepper, a leader of the newly formed League for the Preservation of American Independence. Root, apparently, did not mind conferring with an outspoken irreconcilable and with a man whose organization was diametrically opposed to the League to Enforce Peace. It was by no means an isolated example of his willingness at this time to co-operate for party harmony with the bitterest foes of Wilson's League of Nations.

So far as the revised Covenant was concerned, Root

agreed with Lodge. It was not acceptable. Almost none of the amendments he had suggested had been incorporated satisfactorily. Disappointed as he was, however, Root was not ready to discard the charter. In fact, he would not even ask for further textual changes. Instead of amendments, he would be content with reservations that would express the Senate's understanding of obscure passages and disclaim all obligations to honor objectionable articles. The consent of the other signatories to such changes could be assumed, unless they entered a formal protest during the process of ratification.

Committing the party to the policy of reservations, as distinct from amendments or outright rejection, was Root's major contribution to the battle over the Treaty of Versailles. The plan seems to have been in his mind as early as December 18, 1918, but the chief saleswork was done during two visits to Washington in June 1919. In his stratagem he received staunch support from Lodge and Hays, both of whom regarded it as the surest means of keeping the party united. Even the irreconcilables seemed to accept the plan at this time, although they later deserted.

To provide a documentary foundation for this policy, Root penned a second open letter, this time to Lodge. It was drawn up in consultation with Lodge, Brandegee, and Philander C. Knox, then an irreconcilable Senator. Dated June 21, 1919, it appeared in the press the next day. In it Root argued that the revision of the Covenant had not gone far enough; and he listed many suggestions, mostly his own, that had been ignored. He recognized, however, that the Covenant did contain many desirable features and that, with Europe in chaos, time was vital. He recommended, therefore, that the Senate give its consent, subject to three reservations. One would clarify the withdrawal procedure, one would further safeguard the Monroe Doctrine, and the last would free the United States from any obligation under Article X. On this last point, Root retreated from his position of March 29. Then he proposed to abandon Article X after five years; now he wished to give it up at once.

3. *The Battle in the Senate*

With the publication of his letter to Lodge on June 22, 1919, Root's most important work was done. As a constructive critic, he had devised a formula that would take the United States into the League of Nations; secure, as he thought, the best and discard the worst of the Covenant; enable the Allies to accept these changes without loss of face; and prevent a split in the Republican party. He retired soon thereafter to Clinton, leaving to Lodge and Hays the formidable task of keeping the faithful united behind the plan of reservations in the ensuing battle in the Senate.

The struggle commenced at once. On June 25, 1919, in direct answer to Root's plan, the White House released a cablegram from Wilson calling ratification with reservations the equivalent of rejection. This dogmatic stand the President never really modified. He might have had his way if a vote could have been taken as soon as the treaty was submitted to the Senate on July 10, but that body did not act then. Rather it spun out its deliberations until November 19, during which time the inevitable failures at Paris were pitilessly disclosed, the opportunity for the President to win over the mild reservationists was hopelessly bungled, and the strength of those desiring complete rejection was enormously increased. As public sentiment for the League as drafted gradually ebbed, the nonreservationist position became untenable; and the Root formula, or something like it, offered the best and only chance to attain the larger part of Wilson's goal.

During this prolonged discussion, Root advised and assisted anyone who sincerely backed the reservations policy. He regarded Lodge as such a person. When the Massachusetts Senator, worried lest two mild reservationists break way, wrote on August 15, "I come to you for help and you must not refuse it to me," Root co-operated to the utmost. He sent ingeniously worded letters, as Lodge desired, to Frank B. Kellogg of Minnesota, a close friend, and to LeBaron B. Colt of Rhode Island, a relative stranger. On the other hand, when Kellogg himself and Walter E. Edge of New Jersey, another mild reservationist appealed for guidance, Root was equally responsive.

Root never wavered in his belief that reservations offered the most practical solution for a complex problem. He blamed the long delay on Wilson, for his initial refusal to consult the Senate before drafting the Covenant, for his failure to secure the necessary amendments in March and April, and for his uncompromising attitude upon his return to America. When the President at Salt Lake City, during his Western tour, reiterated his rejection of reservations, Root on September 26, 1919, called him "defiant" and "an awful bluffer." That very day, Wilson collapsed and was hurried back to Washington where he suffered a paralytic stroke. Not once during the long illness that followed did Root commit to paper an expression of sympathy or pity.

For the Senate, in general, Root had nothing but praise. He sensed danger, to be sure, that Lodge, irritated by Wilson's stubbornness, might impose too stringent reservations or that the irreconcilables, scenting the possibility of outright rejection, might go back on their promises. On August 28 and again on September 10, 1919, he warned

Lodge not to allow the extremists to gain control. On November 12, he told Kellogg why the reservations should go so far and no further. If the Allies accepted the treaty with the Senate's reservations, it would expose Wilson as an inept negotiator who had failed to obtain all the safeguards for the United States that the other nations were willing to grant. If, however, because the reservations were too severe, the Allies objected to the Senate's changes, Wilson would be vindicated. It was obvious, Root concluded, that the true friends of the treaty with reservations must not overplay their hand.

On November 19, 1919, the Senate was ready to choose between the Wilson and Root methods of entering the League of Nations. All amendments to the Covenant had been defeated; and fourteen reservations, some important and some trivial, had been inserted in the resolution of ratification. On the first test, the treaty with reservations failed to pass. The tally stood 39 to 55, with almost all of the Democrats and the irreconcilables, who now showed their true colors, in opposition. On the second ballot, the treaty without reservations was also unable to muster a majority. The roll call disclosed 38 in favor and 53 against. Only the Democrats responded aye, while the obstructionist irreconcilables switched over to join the reservationists, strong and mild. With the deadlock complete, the Senate adjourned for a fortnight.

Root manifested no undue disappointment or discouragement over this inconclusive result. He seems to have believed that the issue had been properly joined, that Wilson must now give way, and that some face-saving formula, satisfactory to all, could be found. He commended Lodge's work as "extraordinarily able . . . one of the greatest examples of parliamentary leadership that I have ever known." Lodge, he stated, had given the treaty its only chance of adoption. In this same letter, Root suggested to

Lodge certain alterations in the reservations, but none of them was drastic.

After the first Senate vote, a subtle but perceptible change occurred in Root. He did not lose faith in Lodge, and the two men remained cordial, even when in disagreement. With the irreconcilables, however, there was a distinct cooling; those men had deserted the reservations plan. There were no more conferences with Brandegee or Knox, and within six months their group would look upon Root with suspicion and fear. In December 1919, Root and Taft, whose relations had been rather perfunctory since the former had declined to join the League to Enforce Peace, met on their old terms and henceforth appeared to see eye to eye on the treaty fight.

The last two weeks of January 1920 witnessed sincere but futile attempts to bridge the gap between Republican reservationists and those Democrats who could be induced to forsake the uncompromising Wilson. Root apparently played no part in these negotiations, but he approved of them. He continued to uphold Lodge and insisted that it was Wilson who must yield. He also defended the Senate from criticism, saying it was engaged in "the greatest contest for the integrity of constitutional government which the world had seen since the civil war."

In the weeks before the second Senate vote, Root hoped the treaty with reservations would pass. He wanted to get the subject out of the way before the Presidential election, and he believed it could be done if Wilson were willing. Should the chief executive remain adamant, he told a New York audience on February 19, 1920, then the country must await a Republican administration, which would invite the League members to revise the Covenant and would call a special conference on international law and arbitration.

But Wilson did not yield. Although there was no hope

for the treaty as drafted, he refused to accept the Republican reservations. The question, then, was whether enough Democrats could be prevailed upon to defy his leadership. The answer came on March 19, 1920. About half of the Democratic Senators, almost all of those up for re-election that year, joined the mild and strong reservationists to give the treaty, as modified, a majority but not the necessary two thirds. With the last-ditch Wilsonians and the irreconcilables banding together, the result was 49 to 35. Seven votes stood between the United States and membership in the League of Nations.

4. *The Election of 1920*

Unlike Root, Woodrow Wilson was in no hurry to dispose of the League issue before the Presidential election. With his unbounded but ungrounded faith that the people would rise in their righteous wrath to smite his opponents and with a reasonable hope that the Republicans might yet split wide open on the question, the President welcomed delay. On January 8, 1920, he asked that the coming election be regarded as "a great and solemn referendum."

It is doubtful whether Root had any faith in converting a Presidential canvass into a test vote on the League or, indeed, any fear of the verdict if it should prove possible. But he did wish his party to be consistent. It must declare for the treaty with reservations; otherwise it would expose itself to the charge of having advocated them, as Wilson put it, in order to nullify, not ratify. The platform, in short, must not be written by the irreconcilables.

Root, however, was not planning to attend the Republican Convention. On March 11, 1920, he had accepted an invitation from the League of Nations to serve on a committee of international jurists entrusted with the task of drafting a statute for the new World Court. This duty would take him to The Hague for the summer. Accordingly, on May 14, after another chat with Taft, he wrote to Lodge, urging that the convention's endorsement of the treaty with reservations be "clear and unmistakable." Unless this were done, the Senate's great constitutional triumph would be dismissed as a subterfuge to defeat by indirection what it could not vanquish openly.

Lodge's reply argued for an entirely different policy. The Senator denied reports that the irreconcilables would demand an anti-League plank, but he acquiesced in their insistence that no pledge be given to accept the Covenant with the fourteen reservations. It was enough, wrote Lodge, to condemn Wilson and to praise the Senate for resisting his domination. To go further, to distinguish between different Republican groups in the Senate and to commit the new President to a specific policy, would precipitate a fight in the convention, lead to a new schism, and perhaps throw away what all agreed would be a certain Republican triumph in November.

There is no direct evidence of Root's opinion of Lodge's letter, but subsequent events suggest that he was impressed by the argument. Accordingly, Root seems to have prepared an ambiguous plank praising a league but not the League. It was a kind of "looking both ways" affair, one broad enough to accommodate every shade of Republican opinion. This paper he entrusted to Ogden Mills, who was a candidate for the chairmanship of the resolutions committee in the convention. Just what instructions Root gave to Mills the records do not disclose, but the latter had the draft in his pocket when the Republican hosts gathered in Chicago on June 8, 1920. On that date Root was nearing the shores of Europe.

For three days and two nights the resolutions committee wrangled over a statement on the treaty. A similar battle raged in the Hotel Blackstone at an unofficial steering group meeting attended by Lodge, Mills, Stimson, Borah, Brandegee, Murray Crane, and others. Crane, a former Senator from Massachusetts and a good friend of Taft, led the fight for a clear endorsement of joining the League under the Senate reservations. Lodge, who was both temporary and permanent chairman, objected and threatened to combat the proposal from the floor. At this point reports of what happened vary; but the best evidence is that Mills chose that moment to pull from his pocket the Root draft. It was accepted at once, apparently without any substantial change, by the Blackstone group, by the resolutions committee, and by the convention. As adopted, the official platform stated that the party stood for an association of nations based upon international justice implemented by the development of law, the decision of impartial courts and general international conference whenever peace was threatened. Moreover, it was made clear that the Republicans believed that all this could be accomplished without compromise of national independence and without depriving the people in advance of the power to determine their action in a specific crisis.

Few acts in Root's public career have been more criticized than his part in aiding and abetting the Republican evasion on the League in 1920. It has been cited as a bald attempt to deceive the American people, as an abject surrender to the irreconcilables, and as a prostitution of principle to party. To an ardent Wilsonian, that judgment is valid, but Root was no ardent Wilsonian. He was never enthusiastic about the Covenant, he preferred a very different sort of league, and he had supported the treaty with reservations only because nothing better was available. Irritated by Wilson's refusal to meet him halfway and haunted by the nightmare of 1912, he was content to rebuke the President, laud the Senate, and endorse the general principle of American membership in a vague association of nations. It was not a courageous stand, but it was consistent with his basic beliefs. And it was politically sound.

His duties at The Hague kept Root from playing a major role in the campaign until the last month. His European activity, however, did not pass unnoticed. It influenced Harding and antagonized the irreconcilables. Since the party faithful had presumably turned their backs, for the moment at least, upon the fledgling League, it was a little perplexing to see one of the high priests laboring in behalf of that infant organization. It was even more confusing when Harding, in his bumbling way, suggested that Root's court plan, if grafted upon the Hague tribunal, might be a substitute for the League of Nations itself.

While the anti-League element suspected Root of undoing his own ambiguous plank, the pro-League Republicans feared Harding would repudiate the part calling for membership in an international association. After the acceptance speech of July 22, 1920, Root received several appeals to restrain the candidate, heretofore a strong reservationist, from yielding to the irreconcilables. About August 19, Root cabled a warning to Hays against letting the issue become one of the League versus no league, instead of Wilson's Versailles League versus the Senate's Americanized league. Hays replied with a tentative plan to declare the Versailles League dead, so far as the United States was concerned, and to seek to combine the best parts of the Covenant with the old Hague Court. Root scoffed at this ridiculous suggestion and bluntly warned that the existing League of Nations offered the only feasible vehicle for carrying out the platform promise. Apparently, Root's cablegram struck home; Hays's brainstorm was not heard of again.

There is a touch of irony in the dread which Root's return to the United States in September aroused in the hearts of his former collaborators. How, asked Albert J. Beveridge of Borah, can the voter distinguish between Wilson's League and Root's? Must we, inquired Brandegee of Lodge, accept Wilson's Covenant to secure Root's court? Even more amusing was the panic inspired by the announcement that on October 25, 1920, Harding would lunch at the Union League Club with Root and Hughes present. The irreconcilables and even some strong reservationists were frightened lest Root trap the gullible Harding into some statement friendly to the League.

Actually, these alarms were needless. Root wanted nothing more than to keep his candidate squarely on the capacious Chicago platform, and he realized that he would have to struggle to get that much. By the time he landed in New York on September 26, two things were crystal clear. First, the Republicans were going to win in November no matter what stand they took on the Covenant. Secondly, Harding, like Lodge, was no longer a strong reservationist but was virtually indistinguishable from the irreconcilables. It was, therefore, to remind the nominee of his pro-League backers, not to deceive the electorate or not to snatch victory from the jaws of defeat, that Root joined with thirty other prominent Republicans in a statement released to the press on October 15, 1920. Other signers were Hughes, Stimson, Lowell, Nicholas M. Butler, John G. Hibben, Herbert Hoover, William Allen White, and Henry W. Taft. William H. Taft was to have been included, but he could not be reached in time.

The statement by the thirty-one Republicans was probably drafted by Root in its original form no later than October 9. It underwent revision by Paul D. Cravath, a New

York lawyer friend, and Jacob G. Schurman, still president of Cornell University, while Hays and perhaps George Harvey were consulted. It advised the voters that the surest way to obtain immediate American membership in an association of nations was to elect Harding. The Democratic candidate, it asserted, was committed to the Wilson League and the limitless obligations of Article X. The people would never accept that arrangement. To elect Cox would achieve nothing; only the choice of Harding could bring about positive results.

The idea of such a manifesto was not original with Root. Before his return, several Republican leaders, including Schurman, Lowell and Herbert Hoover, either had recommended it or had actually taken the initial steps. All, however, regarded Root's co-operation as indispensable. On the other hand, none believed the appeal was an absolute necessity for victory; Harding's election was taken for granted. The statement was designed, rather, to serve as a reminder after November 2, 1920, of what the party had promised at Chicago in June. It was directed as much toward the Republican candidate and his friends as toward the voters.

Root's authorship of the October statement, like that of the Chicago platform, has been much criticized as a disingenuous attempt to mislead the people on what they might expect from a Republican administration. It is doubtful, however, whether very many contemporaries who tried between June and November 1920 to follow Harding's meanderings on the Covenant could seriously accept the declaration as a binding promise to enter the League, or even a league. The most the paper could do before the election was to assure one class of voters that there was within the Republican party a group of distinguished Americans who would try to persuade the new President to take some positive action regarding a postwar international organization.

The final contribution made by Root to the so-called great and solemn referendum was an address at Carnegie Hall on October 19, 1920. There he spelled out at length the reasons for his support of Harding and vehemently attacked Article X. It was there, rather than in the Chicago platform or in the statement of the thirty-one Republicans, that Root deserves censure; for he went beyond the bounds of fairness in defining Cox's position and in construing what would be America's commitments under Article X.

In the last analysis, nothing Root said or left unsaid affected the outcome. Harding won easily in a landslide that represented the accumulated grievances against eight years of Wilsonism. The League of Nations was not a decisive issue; its ultimate fate was not the result of the expressed will of the voters but rather of the interpretation the victors chose to place upon their triumph after March 4, 1921.

To loyal Wilsonians, Root's course during the fight over the Treaty of Versailles was unworthy of him. Through such eyes, the distinguished elder statesman, who should have been above petty bickering and maneuvers, appeared as a carping critic, a bitter partisan, and a false advocate. Presumably the friend of a postwar league, Root, they felt, consciously or unconsciously played into the hands of the irreconcilables, the isolationists of the day. Since few, even among Wilsonians, were prepared to call Root a fool, they concluded he must be a knave.

Such an estimate is unjust to Root. He had his blind spots, to be sure; and an implacable dislike of Wilson did not improve his vision in certain directions. He co-operated with the irreconcilables in an effort to bind them to a policy of reservations, and they deserted him when the chips were down. He agreed, in the interest of party unity, to draft an all-inclusive plank; and the men who had insisted upon it were the first to repudiate it. He gave Lodge every possible aid when the Senator was in need and then watched his old friend move away from the position they had shared. Root always maintained that his course during 1918–1920 had been correct, but it is probable that after 1921 he looked back upon those years with some mixed emotions.

The loyal Wilsonians, moreover, tend to forget the incredible blunders their chief committed in his quest for ratification, as well as the sharp break with the past that the Covenant represented. The President violated about every rule in the book of politics, and in his crusade for a new world order he assumed a popular willingness to undertake responsibilities for which the nation was not prepared.

Finally, however much Root may have been governed by pride, prejudice, or party loyalty, his criticism of the Covenant — and it was constructive criticism — and his advocacy of the reservations plan were wholly consistent with his record on the arbitration treaties of 1911 and his attitude toward the League to Enforce Peace during the war. Article X was the line of demarcation in the thinking of Root and Wilson; not until June 1950 did the United States act upon the principle inherent in that much-debated clause. Root, in short, was a transition figure in America's emergence as a world power. He envisaged a peace structure that relied upon arbitration and international law, not armed force and international legislation, to preserve order and stability in the world. The lesson of the postwar years, which he did not live to read completely, was that his formula was not enough.

V I I

Interwar Years:
Elder Statesman   1921-1937

W HEN WARREN G. HARDING took the oath of office
to usher in the Republican restoration, Elihu Root had
passed his seventy-sixth birthday. A new generation of political leaders had emerged. The incoming President was
twenty years Root's junior; Coolidge and Hoover were
even younger. Hence Root did not pay much attention
after election day to the constant speculation about his becoming again Secretary of State. He was neither surprised
nor disappointed when that office went to Charles Evans
Hughes, aged fifty-eight, partly on the ground, as Harding confided to Taft, that "Root was an elder statesman
of a different generation."

The role of elder statesman, which Root was destined to
play from 1921 to 1937, was not a new one for him. Entering public life late, he had always been looked to as
the wise man, dispassionate, imperturbable, perspicacious,
and keenly analytical. Quite naturally, the Presidents of
the 1920's dutifully sought, on occasion, the opinion of
this venerable political sage. But the Root of the interwar
years was not the Root of the Roosevelt era. He was less
active, less energetic and, inevitably, his influence was
slighter. After three quarters of a century his superb physical machine began to run down. In the autumn of 1923

he fell quite ill. A stone was removed from his kidney in January 1924 and full recovery did not come until April. Soon afterward, Mrs. Root, who for ten years had not been robust, took a turn for the worse. She suffered painfully from arthritis; and during a final illness, which culminated on June 8, 1928, her husband's own strength broke temporarily under the strain. It was then that the first signs of a serious heart condition manifested themselves, an ailment which confined him increasingly to his New York apartment and his house in Clinton. By the early 1930's, weakening eyesight severely curtailed his reading, and he grew more and more dependent upon others for information from the printed page. Although his mental faculties remained remarkably active and his memory, for the most part, excellent, it was not surprising that his analysis of developments at home and abroad became less profound as the end drew near.

1.   *The League of Nations*

Although Harding excluded Root from his cabinet, ostensibly because of years, many persons instinctively thought of him as the logical man to head the State Department. Even if age barred a full term, it was appropriate, as Taft kept insisting, to have Root serve until the party's promise to join an association of nations was realized. Who was better fitted by experience and talents to accomplish that delicate task, whether it was done by a commission sent to Europe or by a conference of the powers in Washington, whether it was effected through a revision of the Covenant or through the creation of an entirely new organization?

Root would have accepted, though he did not seek, a

temporary appointment for just the purpose Taft envisaged. But Harding was subjected to pressures that kept
him from making the offer, even if he had been disposed
to do so. The irreconcilables, who were still powerful in
the Senate, disliked Root, while certain strong reservationists, who had shifted their position after March 1920, distrusted him. The apprehensions of these two groups had
been awakened during the last stages of the Presidential
campaign, and they were not quieted after the November
landslide. Lodge, for example, wrote Harding on November 10 and again on December 23 that, despite his long
friendship for Root, he must oppose his appointment so
long as Root believed that the Versailles Treaty, however
modified and amended, offered the only feasible association
of nations.

There were other sources of hostility to Root as Secretary
of State. The Senate bloc which had dictated Harding's
nomination wished to keep the conduct of foreign affairs
in its own hands. It did not desire a strong man like Root
or, for that matter, even one like Hughes. There is also
some evidence that Root's August cablegram, though
solicited by Hays, had been twisted by men close to Harding into an improper attempt to dictate to the candidate.

Much more important to Root than a seat in the Harding cabinet was a solution regarding the League of Nations.
Here his political honesty and acumen were at stake. As
author of the Chicago plank, he had bound his party to
sponsor an international association to promote world
peace. As drafter of the statement by thirty-one prominent Republicans, he had advised the people that the most
effective method to secure America's "full part in an association with the other civilized nations to prevent war"
was to choose Harding over Cox. To be sure, the June resolution did not bear his name, and the October manifesto
was more a prediction than a pledge. Still, Root was per-

sonally involved in the path the new administration picked; and if nothing were done to join a concert of powers, he would be exposed to charges of bad faith, stupidity, or both.

Although little could be accomplished in a positive way until March 4, 1921, several of Root's correspondents were worried by preinaugural developments. On November 4, 1920, Harding declared that, so far as the United States was concerned, "the League is now deceased." On November 20, Lodge repeated, with less circumlocution, "The League is dead." By December 29, even Porter J. Mc-Cumber, originally the sole Republican nonreservationist in the Senate, conceded that an amended Covenant could never pass and that some new organization must be devised. This repudiation of the League, but not necessarily of a league, elicited no protest from Root; for while he personally preferred to build upon a going institution, neither the party platform nor the statement by the thirty-one required membership in the existing League of Nations. Encouraged by the appointment to the cabinet of two of the thirty-one, as against one irreconcilable, Root opposed putting pressure on the President-elect and advised the dissatisfied to be patient.

Patience, however, was not rewarded after Harding took office. Never noted for his luminous prose, the chief executive in his first addresses obscured rather than enlightened. It was reasonably clear that he would not advocate entering the League; but he offered to associate with other nations "for conference, for counsel, to seek the expressed views of world opinion, to recommend a way to approximate disarmament." There is no evidence that Root had any part in preparing these masterpieces of ambiguity.

During the summer of 1921, with its future still undetermined, the nebulous association of nations, which this country might safely join instead of the existing League, was put on the shelf. The administration had decided to sponsor a conference on naval limitations and Far Eastern problems, and on September 21, Harding wrote to Root that he would not raise any other diplomatic question that might jeopardize the success of the gathering.

The unfulfilled assurances of October 1920 were not the only matter connected with the League that embarrassed Root in the summer of 1921. Early in June he had been requested, as one of the four American judges on the Hague Court, to submit names suitable for election by the League Council and Assembly to seats on the new World Court. The invitation had been sent, as a matter of courtesy, via the State Department, at which place it had been inexplicably relegated to a dead file. Despite press announcements and letters from European friends, Root received no request directly until August 14, 1921.

Before Root and his colleagues undertook this useful but hardly onerous task, they had to answer two questions. One concerned authority. Since they were requested to nominate, not as private citizens, but as judges of the Hague tribunal and since they held their positions by appointment of the President, acting under a treaty approved in 1900, could they properly deal with the League of Nations which, in effect, the Senate had refused to join? The second question had to do with expediency. Even if the Hague judges believed they possessed the authority, was it wise to exercise it at this time? In the popular mind, the World Court was the judicial arm of the League. The League was a highly controversial subject. Was it advisable to embarrass the administration on the eve of the arms conference by arousing needlessly the anti-League element in the upper house, the very body which would eventually pass upon the work of that gathering?

Under the circumstances, Root felt obliged to consult

Hughes before acting. The Secretary was not adamant; but he did point out that since Root and his colleagues held Presidential appointments, anything they did would be generally interpreted as a government measure. It was obvious to Root that the State Department preferred that no nominations be made, and he returned to New York to inform his associates. John Bassett Moore yielded willingly, but Oscar S. Straus and George Gray did so with considerable misgiving. In mid-September 1921, Root cabled Geneva that the American members of the Hague Court had reluctantly decided that they were "not entitled to make nominations." Regret over the delay was expressed.

When this episode became known, it was widely interpreted as an example of the Harding administration's hostility to the League of Nations. Both Root and Hughes, who wished the League well, were placed in false positions, ones that encouraged critics to brand their signing the statement of the thirty-one as the rankest hypocrisy. Root never defended himself, but always regarded the incident as sheer bad luck. If the invitations had been received in June, when they were sent, instead of after the calling of the Washington Conference, they could have been complied with; and no slap, real or imaginary, at the League of Nations would have resulted.

With the adjournment of the arms conclave in February 1922, the administration was free again to carry out its promises of 1920. It surprised no one, however, by doing nothing. What was astonishing, at least in retrospect, was the tacit acceptance of this inaction by the thirty-one Republicans. They did not protest, nor did they apologize for having given false assurances. In May 1923, Lowell did correct certain erroneous interpretations that Harding was then putting upon his campaign of three years before; but Root remained silent, realizing, as did many of his countrymen, but not the devout Wilsonians, that for a variety of reasons, some logical and some illogical, American membership in the League of Nations was out of the question and that the European states would not abandon a going institution to start all over again just to please the United States.

Rather than pleading for a lost cause, Root concentrated his efforts upon softening a popular antipathy that made co-operation with the existing League difficult. He was determined that hostility, originating in the party's conflict with Wilson, should not become a permanent tenet of Republicanism. He began his campaign for tolerance in May 1923, and climaxed these pleas for friendly understanding on December 28, 1926, when he received the award, ironically enough, of the Woodrow Wilson Foundation for his contribution to international peace. In accepting the prize, Root declared that the League in the political field and the World Court in the judicial had been "rendering the best service in the cause of peace known to the history of civilization — incomparably the best." During this same period, he charged, the United States had not only refrained from helping but also exhibited shocking bad taste and worse manners. It had uttered no word of sympathy or kindness. It had allowed "insensate prejudice," engendered by domestic factionalism, to misrepresent the true idealism of the American heart. "These, my friends," he concluded, "are some of the evils visited upon us by a hateful and contentious spirit; from which may the good Lord deliver us."

These remarks by Root can be taken as his final thoughts during the 1920's on the League of Nations. They must not be construed as an apology for the course he had pursued during the peacemaking or even as a subsequent regret over the abstention of the United States. At the end of 1926, Root did not propose outright membership. What he condemned was the temper of American policy and of public opinion after the Covenant had been rejected. What he deplored was the lack of friendliness and of a willingness to co-operate wherever compatible with freedom of action.

2. *The Washington Conference*

While the League remained a symbol and a touchstone in interwar diplomacy, other and more pressing problems came to the fore. First in point of time was the Conference on the Limitation of Armament, held in Washington from November 12, 1921, to February 6, 1922, and in which Root participated as one of the four American delegates.

This conference was a milestone in American foreign relations. It imposed certain restrictions upon naval construction and prohibited the further fortification of several overseas bases. It established a new relationship between four major powers in the Pacific area and erected machinery for settling future disputes among them. It wrote into international law the traditional policy of the United States toward China and gave that strife-torn land a chance, on paper at least, to put its house in order. It inaugurated a period of cordiality with Japan which lasted, despite a severe blow in 1924, for nine years. It encouraged the State Department to make further efforts, at Geneva in 1927 and at London in 1930, to set additional curbs on the world's fleets. Widely approved in 1922, the work of the Washington Conference fell into disfavor in the 1930's and, after Pearl Harbor, was condemned as a blunder of the first magnitude.

The selection of Root was logical and, perhaps, inevitable. Each nation was allowed four representatives, and

Harding decided to name three Republicans and one Democrat. He was determined to avoid Wilson's mistakes of omitting eminent figures and of ignoring the Senate. Hughes, as Secretary of State, became the chairman of the delegation. The leader of each party in the upper house, Lodge and Oscar W. Underwood, were chosen to facilitate approval by that body. For the remaining spot, Harding saw the wisdom of honoring the party's outstanding authority on foreign affairs and at the same time of mollifying the followers of the thirty-one. Root's appointment was announced on September 10, 1921.

To his new task, Root brought certain useful ideas. Although willing to go along with the overwhelming popular demand for a drastic reduction in naval expenditures, he was no doctrinaire like Borah. After all, he had been too closely associated with Theodore Roosevelt and too ardent a champion of preparedness from 1915 to 1917 to cut the fleet beyond the margin of safety. On the other hand, some curb on excessive armaments would relieve international tensions, especially in the Far East. Realizing the impossibility of measuring national needs afloat to the satisfaction of all parties, Root suggested reductions in proportion to the existing strength of the navies affected. This idea, which proved to be the vital formula for success, apparently occurred independently to both Root and Hughes.

Root also acted upon a realistic appraisal of what was possible. He did not bemoan the abandonment of vessels that were obsolete or of blueprints that would never materialize. For him, the sacrifice the United States might make in scrapping ships on the ways or in accepting restrictions upon the further fortification of the Philippines bore a direct relation to the likelihood of obtaining huge Congressional appropriations for the naval establishment. The gap between legislative promise and performance,

especially with regard to the Pacific outposts, Root remembered only too clearly from his days in the War Department. Hence, at one of the preliminary meetings of the
American delegation in October, he extracted from Lodge
and Underwood their considered and pessimistic opinion
of what Congress might and might not do.

Of all the American commissioners, Root was the most
friendly toward Japan. He was influenced by vestiges of a
pre-Portsmouth sentiment and by the pride he took in having reached an understanding on immigration and other
matters in 1908–1909. To be sure, he was bothered by
some of Japan's subsequent actions, particularly the
Twenty-one Demands of 1915; but he accepted at face
value the Nipponese assurances regarding the mandated
Marshall, Caroline and Marianas Islands, as well as the
pledges to return Shantung to China and eastern Siberia to
Russia. Actually, Japan's performance at the conference
and for some years afterward justified Root's trust.

It is difficult, if not impossible, to assess accurately Root's
specific contribution to the proceedings. There is no doubt
that Hughes dominated the American delegation and that
Root gracefully accepted his leadership. Certain jobs were
purposely assigned by the secretary to his colleagues, and
to Root fell the task of sponsoring a treaty to govern the
operation of submarines in future wars. He also had a
hand in drafting the Nine-Power agreement on China;
and he did what he could, sometimes going beyond the
wishes of the State Department, to mediate between Japan
and China over Shantung. But neither the Four-Power
nonaggression pact nor the Five-Power Treaty on naval
tonnage and naval bases owed very much to his efforts.

In his estimate of the Washington Conference, Root
shared the satisfaction and optimism of most of his contemporaries. He did say to his biographer in 1931 that
"the Conference was the complete negation of naval pol-

icy"; but by that he meant that the civilian statesmen and not the admirals had made the basic decisions. There is no reason to interpret that remark, as it sometimes has been, to imply that he regarded the Washington treaties as disastrous to national security. On February 18, 1922, he praised the agreements to Stimson as the first steps ever taken to abandon a policy among nations of competitive force, and he listed as the supreme achievement the spirit of mutual trust and confidence that had been engendered. Two months later he publicly declared, with respect to the Four-Power Pact, "I doubt if any formal treaty ever accomplished so much by doing so little." He hailed the benefits to China, the improvement in Japanese-American relations, and the strengthening of international law. He was not bothered by the scrapping of hulls and the restrictions upon the defenses of Guam and the Philippines, for he understood that the United States Navy had lost nothing that it had any reasonable chance of obtaining. From the little evidence available, it appears that Root was sympathetic to Secretary of State Stimson's efforts in 1930 to extend at London the Washington limitations to other types of naval craft. He did not live to see the nation react against this policy begun so hopefully in 1921–1922.

3. The World Court

The most constant and absorbing of Root's interests in the interwar years was the Permanent Court of International Justice. Membership in such a tribunal had long been an objective of American diplomacy, and Root was partly responsible for that fact. As Secretary of State, he had in 1907 drawn the necessary plans and had instructed the American delegates to the Hague Conference to secure their approval. In 1919 and 1920, Root's major criticism of the Covenant, aside from Article X, was that it gave insufficient attention to the judicial functions of the League and minimized the role of arbitration. Root was also one of the drafters of the statute defining the powers of the new World Court and had spent the summer of 1920 at The Hague helping to draw up the basic document. As a result of his labors, he was widely urged in 1921 to accept a seat on the court; but he firmly refused, alleging age and an unwillingness to transplant himself and his wife to Holland.

Although he hoped that the United States would quickly join the World Court, Root realized that some delay was unavoidable. The passions aroused in the Senate by the League fight must be allowed to subside, while tension in the Pacific and the race in naval construction required prior consideration. Hence he accepted without protest the Hughes strategy of disposing of the Washington Conference before pressing for adherence to the court. He was rewarded in February 1923, when Harding submitted to the Senate a plan to bring the United States into the World Court. Hughes was the guiding spirit; the President acquiesced if only because the scheme provided another justification for forgetting the proposed association of nations. Since the chief argument against entering the court was its tie with the League, four reservations were appended that would secure for this country the same rights as the members of the League without, however, becoming entangled in League affairs.

Root, apparently, did not object to these conditions. In the spring of 1923 he joined Hughes and Secretary of Commerce Hoover in a drive to stir up Congressional and popular sentiment for the administration's proposal. He made one major address at Washington on April 26 and simultaneously tried, vainly it turned out, to persuade

Lodge that the Hughes reservations insured American equality on every essential point. A year later, the platforms of both major parties endorsed the World Court, although a draft by Root, prepared at Coolidge's request, proved to be too forthright to satisfy all shades of Republican opinion. But Lodge as chairman of the Senate Committee on Foreign Relations, and also his successor, Borah, resisted administration pressure for prompt action. Almost three years elapsed before the recommendations of February 1923 came to a vote.

During this interval, the opponents of the World Court discovered another danger, more fatal, presumably, than the connection with the League. This one concerned the advisory opinions that were furnished, on request, to the Council and the Assembly. This practice, precedent for which can be found in American state governments, was deemed objectionable on two grounds. First, as the United States was not represented in the Council or Assembly, it was unable to oppose, as others could, requests for advisory opinions. Second, the court in these opinions might discuss certain issues, such as the Monroe Doctrine or immigration laws, which most Americans believed were not subject to international jurisdiction. Although advisory opinions had no force of law and bound no one, it was alleged that mere discussion might embarrass the United States and must, therefore, be prevented.

Accordingly, a fifth reservation was proposed, asserting that the United States would pay no heed to advisory opinions on questions not submitted by herself. When consulted by Coolidge on this point in May 1925, Root raised no objection. The alarmists, however, wanted something stronger and eventually won. By the substitute fifth reservation, the World Court would be barred from rendering an advisory opinion on any matter in which the United States claimed an interest and which it did not wish considered. In short, the United States would not be bound by such judgments and it could even prevent them from being delivered.

With five reservations appended, the Senate on January 27, 1926, approved a bill to enter the World Court. The vote was 76 to 17. Would the other members accept these conditions? Root felt they should; in July 1926 he wrote to Lord Phillimore, a co-worker at The Hague in 1920, that the reservations were designed simply to give the United States equal rights. The other powers did not agree. They were willing to consent to the four original reservations and that part of the fifth which permitted the United States an opportunity to oppose a request for an advisory opinion. But they could not allow the Americans to prohibit the judges from acting, for no other member of the tribunal possessed that veto. They suggested, therefore, that this problem be the subject of further negotiation. Coolidge, however, insisted that the Senate's terms be accepted *in toto* and on November 11, 1926, announced, in effect, that the court plan had been dropped.

The evidence on Root's views of this unexpected development is scanty. We do know that he minimized the danger that the fifth reservation was designed to forestall and that he felt the whole affair had been mismanaged. In October 1926, he was pessimistic about the future of American membership and believed that only a Democratic victory in 1928 could bring it about.

As a matter of fact, little was done for over two years. During that interval Secretary of State Kellogg, prodded by French diplomacy and overborne by American opinion, negotiated a treaty by which fifteen countries — later sixty-five — promised to renounce war as an instrument of policy and to settle all disputes by peaceful means. Root was not responsible in any way for the Kellogg-Briand Pact. He was consulted during the negotiations but only because a new arbitration treaty with France was being drafted simultaneously.

Within limits, Root endorsed this experiment in peace. He declared that the treaty set a simple, clear standard of conduct that all nations could comprehend and accept. Unlike the Covenant, it did not attempt to do too much, nor did it require military power for enforcement. The strength of public opinion or public condemnation, he believed, would be sufficient to uphold the pact. There was no need for clarifying reservations by the Senate. The agreement, moreover, would help dispel European resentment against the United States for its recent economic policies and for its abstention from various endeavors for peace. Root did not expect to obtain all the benefits claimed by the zealous champions of the outlawry of war, and he did fear that the pact might lull the people into a sense of false security. But, consistent with his attitude toward Article X, he did not criticize what seems today the most evident flaw, the absence of machinery to prevent and to punish violations.

The conclusion of the Kellogg Pact, with its promise to settle all disputes by peaceful means, raised anew the question of the World Court. In November 1928, Coolidge hinted that the deadlock of two years before might soon be broken. A month later, the League Council decided to assemble a new committee of jurists to revise the statute of 1920. An invitation was extended, perhaps only out of courtesy, to Root; but he surprised and delighted his friends by accepting with alacrity. On his eighty-fourth birthday, a chill February day, he started across the wintry Atlantic for Geneva.

As in 1920, Root acted as a private citizen. He held no government appointment. This time, however, with a friendly administration in office, he conferred with the President, the Secretary of State, and influential Senators before leaving. He also carried with him the good wishes of President-elect Hoover, a staunch supporter of the World Court. Although ironing out snarls over the fifth reservation was not his major purpose, Root hoped to find some way out of the existing impasse.

The committee convened on March 11, 1929, and adjourned eight days later with the statute revised and a compromise on advisory opinions effected. This last, usually known as the Root formula (although others had a hand in it), set up machinery by which the United States could register its opposition to any request for an advisory opinion on questions in which it claimed an interest. If, after discussion, the majority of the members of the court continued to demand a judgment, then the United States might quit the tribunal "without any imputation of unfriendliness or unwillingness to co-operate generally for peace and goodwill."

In hammering out this cumbersome procedure, Root was not as cautious as he should have been. He regarded American fears over advisory opinions as baseless; and he paid insufficient heed to suggestions and warnings cabled by the State Department, suggestions to eliminate advisory opinions altogether and warnings that his draft did not cover everything the Senate had required in 1926. It was clear to many observers that the Senatorial foes would take advantage of and exploit these shortcomings.

For the moment, however, this danger was discounted. The legendary reputation of Root, the prestige of the new Hoover administration, the enthusiasm generated by the Kellogg Pact, and the tranquil nature of the world situation encouraged a belief that the compromise would be accepted. And so it probably would have been if action could have been taken in the summer of 1929. But another interminable delay ensued. The protocol was not submitted to the Senate until twenty months after Root's return, and it took more than four additional years for that body to reach a vote. Recalcitrant legislators were chiefly responsible for this procrastination, but Hoover and Franklin D. Roosevelt must bear some of the blame. Both Presidents favored joining the World Court; but each, at different times, subordinated the project to more pressing domestic and foreign measures.

Whatever its causes, this prolonged delay was fatal. The favorable conditions at home and abroad vanished. The onset of the depression robbed Hoover of his prestige and turned American eyes inward. By 1935, Japan and Germany had quit the League, Hitler had torn up part of the Versailles Treaty, the World Disarmament Conference had failed, and Mussolini's legions were poised to strike at helpless Ethiopia. These developments caused a resurgence of isolationism in the United States, one that was fed by bitterness over defaulted war debts, by recriminations against bankers and munitions makers, and by dread over involvement in a new European holocaust. The World Court dealt itself a serious blow in 1931 by prohibiting an Austro-German customs union. To many unbiased people, this opinion seemed to stem from political considerations rather than judicial reasoning.

During this exasperating period, Root maintained a serenity, patience, and optimism that marked his last years. Perhaps he realized how powerless he was to alter events. In the summer of 1929 he urged Secretary of State Stimson to move as quickly as possible, but he never questioned Hoover's decision to wait, and he rarely criticized Franklin D. Roosevelt's refusal to insist upon speed. He corresponded with Senators of all points of view, but his influence was obviously not what it had been in 1919. On January 21, 1931, just before his eighty-sixth birthday, he was the sole witness at a hearing before the Senate Foreign Relations Committee. For an hour and a

half he read from and commented upon a prepared statement; for another sixty minutes he answered questions.
All in all, it was a remarkable performance for a man of his
age.

To the end, Root remained cautiously hopeful. But he
and Roosevelt badly underestimated the strength of the
court's foes, and tactical mistakes were made. Over the
week end of January 26–27, 1935, a vindictive Hearst
press and the blatant Father Coughlin unleashed an ava-
lanche of telegrams that frightened wavering Senators into
opposition. On the evening of January 28, Root was
routed from bed to help suggest concessions; and his views
were delivered the next morning to the White House. But
these moves were too little and too late. On January 29, the
protocol received a vote of 52 to 36, seven short of the
necessary two thirds. Two attempts to join the court had
failed; there would not be another until after Root's
death and a second world war.

4. *Domestic Affairs*

As an elder statesman, Root continued to manifest a
keen interest in domestic affairs, but with the passing of
the years his judgment became less acute and his influence
negligible. In politics he never faltered in his staunch
Republicanism. He felt free to oppose its leaders on one
matter, the Eighteenth Amendment; but through triumph and defeat, calm and turmoil, prosperity and depression, he regarded his party as the embodiment of sane
conservatism and governmental wisdom. Not even the
scandals of the Harding era daunted him. In a birthday
speech in 1925, he went out of his way to assert that
"there has been no period in the life of the American Re-

public in which she has been served by abler men, answering to higher standards of conduct . . . than she is today."

Advancing years did not soften Root's judgments of political foes. The Progressives of 1924, with their talk of judicial reform, seemed to him a reincarnation of the Bull Moosers; and he described La Follette as "a pretty weak imitation of Roosevelt with a little French Revolution thrown in." The Republican insurgents of 1926 resembled those of 1910. He respected John W. Davis in 1924 and Al Smith in 1928, but felt that both were superior to their party. For the New Deal he had nothing but scorn. Like the New Freedom that had frustrated his Senatorial career, it exploited, in his opinion, a national emergency to broaden the powers of the central government and to infringe upon individual liberties and private property.

Toward the occupants of the White House, Root had mixed feelings. None excited the affection he felt for McKinley or Roosevelt; none aroused the hatred with which he regarded Wilson. With Harding, relations were cordial but not intimate. Root accepted the Ohioan for what he was — an amiable, well-intentioned third-rater. He always remembered their first important contact. In making the nominating speech for Taft at Chicago in 1912, Harding committed the unpardonable blunder of mentioning his candidate's name before the concluding sentence. With pandemonium raging and a carefully prepared manuscript half unread, he turned to Root, the presiding officer, and asked whether there was any way to check the demonstration. Root stared at him with incredulity and blurted out, "My God, man, do you want to stop it?" After 1923, Root's recorded comments on the Harding tragedy were conspicuously absent.

Like so many of his contemporaries, Root held Coolidge in high esteem. He admired his directness, approved his financial policies, and applauded his resistance to the liberal elements within the party. He did not seem to be bothered by the Vermonter's ingrained provincialism in foreign affairs; and on one occasion, in a perfunctory speech, he went so far as to liken Coolidge to Theodore Roosevelt.

Of all the postwar Republican chieftains, Root regarded Hoover as the ablest and the most courageous. He regretted his stand on the liquor question in 1928, but believed that his record as an organizer and as an executive made him the best-equipped candidate in many years. The two men saw eye to eye on foreign policy and on the dangers of government regulation. Root accepted the Hoover contention that the depression had been overcome by 1932 and that only the prospect of a Democratic administration prevented full recovery at that time.

About Franklin D. Roosevelt, Root left little on paper, but it is not difficult to guess what his opinion was of that man.

The domestic question that most aroused Root was the Eighteenth Amendment. He objected to it on personal, political, and legal grounds. A moderate drinker himself, he resented this invasion of his personal rights. He denied the power of the Federal government to regulate such matters, and he warned that his party was playing with political dynamite. In March 1920 he appeared before the Supreme Court and urged that the amendment be declared null and void. Root always opposed constitutional change, and he had little sympathy for reformers. The fanaticism of most drys disgusted him, and he did not conceal his contempt.

Upon the social problems of the 1920's Root's record was uneven. On the one hand, he denounced the Ku Klux Klan and ridiculed the Fundamentalist attack in the Scopes trial on the teaching of evolution. On the other, he supported, for the most part, the stringent immigration laws of the decade, endorsed the racist theories of Madison Grant, and fought a Federal child-labor amendment. This last problem, he argued, should be dealt with by the states. His stand on the Sacco-Vanzetti case is not clear. He helped to finance the publication of the official record and offered suggestions regarding the prefatory material. Yet never once did he publicly protest against the treatment the men received; and, if Nicholas Murray Butler's recollection was correct, Root said in 1929 that the Italians had been fairly tried and that the evidence of their guilt was overwhelming.

It was not to be expected that after his seventy-sixth birthday Root would play an active or decisive role in domestic affairs. He was in the postwar years more a symbol of principles than a maker of policies — a conservative Republican who recalled the McKinley era. In the realm of foreign relations, Root's significance in the interwar years is also to be found in what he stood for, rather than in what he did. He embodied the cautious concern for world peace that had been held by many Republicans before 1914. After 1921 there was no marked change in his approach to internationalism. A peace structure grounded on armed force was still anathema to him, and pledges to uphold the territorial integrity and political independence of another country were still as unpalatable as they had been in Article X.

But Root supported with all his heart the compromise with Wilsonism sponsored by Harding, Coolidge, and Hoover. He wanted to have his cake and eat it too, to enjoy both freedom of action and some collective security. He favored co-operation with the League of Nations, full participation in the World Court, and consultative pacts for areas of vital interest. He was willing to experiment with the limitation of naval armaments and even with a simple promise to renounce war. The codification of international law, the revision of the rules of maritime warfare, and the development of arbitration remained a constant aim.

In other diplomatic matters, Root clung to positions he had assumed in the past. He never seemed ready to grant independence, bruited about since 1900, to the Philippines; and in 1927 he defended American activity in Nicaragua much as he would have done a quarter of a century earlier. His faith in the reasonableness of Japan persisted, and he talked as though the gentlemen's agreement and the Root–Takahira understanding constituted a proper solution for all problems of the 1920's. He was shocked and saddened by the needless affront to Japan in the Immigration Act of 1924, and during the early stages of the Manchurian invasion of 1931 he reminded Stimson of Tokyo's undoubted rights and probable provocation in that province. Fortunately, perhaps, for his peace of mind, Root died before Nippon embarked upon an all-out conquest of China in July 1937. By then both the League of Nations and the World Court had been proved inadequate to cope with the uninhibited force of the dictators; the fabric of his revered international law had been torn to shreds; and, at home, the spirit of the irreconcilables was, for the moment at least, resurgent and triumphant.

VIII

Appraisal:

The Man and His Times

On FEBRUARY 7, 1937, on the eve of his ninety-second birthday, Root died of bronchial pneumonia. A fortnight's illness had sapped his strength; and his three children, summoned in advance, were at his bedside in the New York apartment. Two days later, after simple ceremonies in the Hamilton College chapel, he was buried on the hill at Clinton, overlooking his beloved valley of the Mohawk, midst scenes cherished by him and by his father before him.

1. What Manner of Man?

The personality and character of Elihu Root were not complex. In fact, he always prided himself on being direct, frank, and aboveboard. He was not, however, an easy man to know well; and any evaluation of his salient traits will vary with the degree of intimacy enjoyed by the appraiser. To his close associates, Root was gracious, generous, companionable, and just, a constant source of advice and inspiration, a symbol of wisdom, truth, and great honor. To those who knew him less well, he appeared reserved, rigid, dispassionate, and impartial, intolerant of sham or stupidity, the inhumanly cold personification of sheer intellect. To his enemies and his critics, he seemed shrewd, arrogant, ruthless, and morally blind, adept at legalistic quibbling, an attorney whose superior talents were available to any client for any case. A cautious, capable, and compelling man, he could neither be ignored nor regarded with indifference.

Root had a powerful mind and a persuasive manner that forced people to yield to his arguments and to follow his counsel. Incisive, witty, and urbane, he could strip issues of the unessential, get to the main point quickly, and devise, with what appeared to be unanswerable logic, original and reasonable solutions. Skilled in the art of human relations, he had a positive genius for reconciling the irreconcilable. Even those who disliked and distrusted him freely admitted his ability to conciliate conflicting views.

Root could lead others because he was able to control himself. There was something puritanical in his self-discipline, in the tight rein he kept on his feelings, and in the stern suppression of any outward show of affection. On the surface, at least, he was undemonstrative, unemotional, and unexcitable, usually unsentimental, and always unruffled. He demanded much of his subordinates; but they worshiped him because of his loyalty, his fairmindedness, and his willingness to drive himself even harder than he did them.

Yet there was another side of the man that the public rarely glimpsed. Within the privacy of his family and close friends, he was playful, gentle, sensitive, and understanding. He was fond of children and loved youth. He could be moved to tears on such occasions as Roosevelt's farewell dinner at the White House in 1909. He delighted in both mixed company and male companionship. He drank and smoked (he once asked a nonsmoker what he did to smell like a man), he relished good stories, and he enjoyed the outdoors, particularly for riding and hunting. An indefatigable worker when aroused, he began after 1912, understandably, to slacken his pace, a change which prompted Taft to accuse him of laziness and an unwillingness to face unpleasant situations.

It is true that often in his public career Root had to be prodded into action or enlisted in a cause by others, by Stimson, Lodge, Taft, or Will Hays. But it is not true that either in his private or public life Root shirked disagreeable tasks. He had a stern sense of duty. If something he deemed right and essential needed to be done, he would undertake it himself, regardless of the personal consequences. His defense of Boss Tweed in 1871, his vindication of the army in the Philippines against all manner of charges from 1899 to 1904, his public reprimand in 1901 of the politically influential General Miles, and his denunciation in 1906 of the politically dangerous William Randolph Hearst all attest to his high courage and utter fearlessness. The most painful instance of devotion to duty came at Chicago in 1912, when he opposed and eventually thwarted the man he loved more than anyone else. Such independence was possible only for one who was intellectually confident, financially secure, and wholly indifferent to popular esteem.

Root combined a curious mixture of modesty and pride. Because he was politically unambitious, he could be a loyal subordinate and yield the headlines to others. On the eve of the treaty fight in 1919, he could tell Stimson sincerely, though mistakenly, that no one cared about his views; but there modesty was reinforced by bitter memories of the rejected New York constitution of 1915. By outliving all his contemporaries, Root could have had the last word on bygone controversies; but he repeatedly refused to write an autobiography. One reason, he told Mark Sullivan in 1927, was that "every now and then I see accounts by this, that and the other man, of how he did the things which I have always supposed I did myself and I could not write a story about those things without appearing to be making a claim on my own account, which is the last thing that I want to do."

On the other hand, Root liked to be consulted and, quite naturally, was pleased when his advice prevailed. In fact, he so much enjoyed being a power behind the throne that he has been accused of wishing to wield authority without bearing the responsibility. Such a charge does not fit a man of his initiative and self-assurance. If he rarely held elective office, it was because his earlier professional practice had made him vulnerable to demagogic attacks and because he lacked the ability to inspire multitudes, rather than because he was timid, irresolute, and afraid to be held to account.

His critics, however, are nearer the truth when they scoff at the statement that Root never allowed personal feelings to sway his judgment, or pride of authorship to influence his thinking. Certainly some of his opposition to the Covenant, in its original and amended form, can be attributed to a belief that he could have done the job better and to the fact that his advice had been ignored.

By the average liberal and reformer of the twentieth century Root was regarded, with some justice, as the epitome of conservatism. Such persons disapproved of his social theories, distrusted his motives, and usually disagreed with his politics. Anti-imperialists like Moorfield Storey, muckrakers like Lincoln Steffens, pacifists like Jane Addams, progressives like Herbert Croly, philosophers like Morris Cohen, Jeffersonians like Josephus Daniels, and foes of bigness like Louis Brandeis, thought of him only as an iron-willed corporation lawyer, who fought constitutional change and social experimentation, who upheld colonialism, militarism, and *laissez faire,* and who always managed to identify principles with party loyalty.

At times, Root was able, by intimate contact, partially to destroy that image. In 1917, Charles E. Russell, Fabian socialist, exposer of the Beef Trust, champion of Irish independence, and all-around reformer was a member of the Russian mission. Ten years earlier, in an ex parte analysis of the origins of some American fortunes, entitled *Lawless Wealth,* Russell had had occasion to speak harshly of Root. During their travels to and from the land of revolution, Root dissipated this initial suspicion and gained a friend with whom he later maintained an affectionate correspondence. When in 1933 Russell wrote his autobiography, he paid high tribute to Root's courage and character.

One of Root's foremost weapons in disarming the suspicious, persuading the reluctant, and reconciling the divided was his ready and irrepressible wit. Few statesmen have possessed a keener sense of humor; fewer still have given it freer scope. By a terse endorsement Root could transform a routine paper into a source of enjoyment, and by an apt anecdote or a play on words he could shorten an interminable argument. His gayest jokes are associated with two men who always delighted in a good laugh, even at their own expense, Roosevelt and Taft.

In 1905, Root pinned this chit on a formal letter of condolence prepared in the State Department for President Roosevelt's signature:

I observe that you are writing to His Royal Highness Adolphe, Grand Duke of Luxemburg, as follows:

"It is with deep sorrow that I learn of the great affliction which has befallen Your Royal Highness, and I offer you my sincere and heartfelt sympathy."

Nothing could be more absolute and unqualified than my belief in your absolute sincerity and truthfulness, and this prompts me to inquire whether the depth of your emotion and the poignancy of your sorrow will interfere with our meeting this evening.

During the preparations for the Jamestown Exposition in 1907, a minor official complained to Root that housing accommodations were wholly inadequate for the diplomatic corps. "Why, Mr. Secretary," he said, "the hotel is so small that I have got to put the Italian Ambassadress in the same room with the Italian Ambassador!" "Of course you can't do that," shot back Root. "Why not put her in the room with the French Ambassador?"

Root was always amused by two of Roosevelt's most characteristic traits, his moralizing and his strenuosity. When the President resorted to platitudes, Root would observe gravely, "The thing I most admire about you, Theodore, is your discovery of the Ten Commandments." When the chief executive passed on for criticism one of his more verbose messages to Congress, Root told him: "Your mental powers are failing. A really active president would have much more than 63 pages." But it was Roosevelt's repeated defense of the Panama affair — a defense in which Root concurred — that prompted the most famous sallies. Once, when the President was holding forth on the subject at even greater length than usual, the Secretary interjected, "Oh, sir, do not let so great an achievement suffer from any taint of legality." Upon another occasion, Roosevelt presented his brief and then glared around the table at his cabinet, saying, "Have I answered the charges? Have I defended myself?" At which point Root answered suavely, "You certainly have, Mr. President. You have shown that you were accused of seduction and you have conclusively proved that you were guilty of rape."

The massive frame of William Howard Taft, normal weight over 300 pounds, offered a perfect target for Root's jocular shafts. His best-known mot came in 1903, when the governor general of the Philippines was seriously ill with amoebic dysentery. Seeking relief, he fled to the mountains, making the last twenty-five mile climb on horseback. When he reported that he had stood the trip splendidly, Root was relieved and amused. With visions of an exhausted nag before him, he hurriedly cabled back the solicitous inquiry, "How is the horse?" Eleven years later a politically wiser but corpulently unchanged Taft received the same treatment. Knowing that the former President summered at Murray Bay in Quebec, Root wrote: "I had begun to fear that you had been pressed into the Canadian contingent for the war in Europe and I thought we should never see you again, because if you ever got on the firing line it would be just almost impossible for the Germans to miss you."

Sturdy as was his character, compelling as was his personality, keen as was his wit, Root's chief asset was an alert, agile, acute, and resourceful mind. He could master a wide array of facts, often intricate and technical, and present them in a logical order that overwhelmed an adversary. His memory was phenomenal. Above all, he was a wise man to whom people instinctively turned for sage counsel and sound advice. He was not a speculative thinker, but for analyzing concrete problems he was unequalled. He was a skillful advocate and a superb defender.

Impressed by Root's irrefutable logic, his factual knowledge, and his confident air, contemporaries were inclined to give him more credit than he deserved in the field of scholarship. His service on the boards of many educational, artistic, and scientific institutions encouraged this belief. Actually, he was not a specialist in international or constitutional law. He was not a constructive jurist; and had he ever sat on the Supreme Court, he would have been more interested in reaching an agreement among the majority than in delivering stimulating opinions. He was a

conciliator and would have been at his best in the Phila-
delphia Convention of 1787, where compromises were
imperative. He would have been better at drawing up a
charter of government, like the Constitution, than at com-
posing an article of faith, like the Declaration of Independence. He was interested in means, not ends, in making
democracy work, not in elaborating its creed.

At the level of an amateur, Root revealed a deep interest
in history, geography, art, and natural science. His reading, however, lacked the voracious quality of Theodore
Roosevelt; and his knowledge wanted the scholarly attributes of Henry Cabot Lodge. He held firm religious convictions, but did not make a parade of them. His outlook was
essentially optimistic, for he never experienced real adversity. He was not one, however, to work out any law of
progress. He loved nature and was happiest when he super-
vised the trees and the planting on his estate at Clinton. He
was, of course, "a lawyer first and all the time"; but he was
also fascinated by the drama of American politics. He did
not possess the voice or showmanship to be a great orator,
but on occasions his speeches were remarkably effective. He
was not a gifted writer; but he composed with facility and
cogency legal briefs, administrative orders, and statements
of party policy.

2. *A Man and His Friends*

In the course of a long life, Root formed with many
prominent Americans friendships that threw light upon
his character, influenced his career, and shaped the history of his times. Most of them were conservative, Republican, well-to-do, and socially correct rather than socially prominent. Many were lawyers, a few, like Andrew

Carnegie, multimillionaires. His first professional idol and long-time associate was Joseph H. Choate. His first political benefactors on the national scene were Chester A. Arthur and William McKinley. His earliest cabinet intimate was John Hay.

This last bond was one of short duration and contrasting temperaments. Hay was sensitive, pessimistic, and given to self-pity; a poet by nature and versatile in his talents; unable to conceal his thoughts, to get along with Senators, or fully to comprehend Roosevelt. Root was tough-skinned, optimistic, and not given to self-analysis; an advocate by disposition and more restricted in his range of abilities; unmatched in keeping his mouth shut, in handling lawmakers, and in restraining or guiding the Rough Rider. Hay always wished Root to succeed him in the State Department, but did not live to see his wish come true.

The most significant of Root's friendships, so far as the nation was concerned, were with Roosevelt, Taft, and Lodge. The tie with Roosevelt was the oldest and most cherished. By training, Root was more like Taft, in temperament, more like Lodge; but his heart belonged to Theodore. If there was any tragedy in Root's life, it was the irreparable breach after 1912.

It is difficult to say which friend needed the other the more. For two decades after they first met in 1881, Root was the benefactor. To him Roosevelt partly owed his initial term in the state legislature, the opportunity to run for mayor, and the nomination for the governorship. Then in 1900 Root rejected and Roosevelt accepted second place on the Republican ticket. A year later an assassin's bullet upset the familiar pattern and cast the younger man in the leading role in the drama of the times. To the everlasting credit of both, this shift in fortunes did not alter their old relationship. The extent to which the new President relied upon Root has been emphasized above, and the steps which led to the fateful split in 1912 have also been chronicled.

The self-inflicted wounds of that year never healed. After Roosevelt's death, Root frequently asserted that, starting in 1916, the old-time cordiality had been restored, that Roosevelt had resumed the practice of submitting for criticism drafts of forthcoming speeches. Certainly after 1919 Root acted as if there had never been a rift. He attended the funeral services at Oyster Bay, delivered two memorial addresses such as he might have made in 1909, contributed a glowing, self-effacing analysis of Roosevelt's foreign policy to a volume in the collected works, and served faithfully on committees of the Roosevelt Memorial Association. The judgments he rendered in his reminiscent letters after 1930 to his own official biographer were extremely fair. In short, Root overcame, as neither he nor Stimson in August 1912 had believed possible, the shock and chagrin aroused by Roosevelt's bitter attack upon him at the Progressive Convention of that year.

Whatever Root may have said or thought, the evidence is overwhelming that there was no comparable forgiveness by Roosevelt. Even the reconciliation with Taft seems to have been more complete. Why Roosevelt remained so unbending is a problem that is of more concern to his biographer than to Root's, but a few guesses may be hazarded. Roosevelt always expected more of Root than of Taft. In retrospect, the split between Roosevelt and his successor may have come to seem inevitable, but not so the alignment of Root with Roosevelt's foes. Root could have stayed out of the convention fight, as Lodge did; but Taft could not. Moreover, Roosevelt and Root were potential rivals for the Republican nomination in 1916. As for the issues raised by the World War and the League of Nations, the colonel assumed that Root would agree with him, whereas no such assumption was made in the case of

Taft. Hence he was more irritated both by Root's reluctance to speak out unreservedly on the issues of the war
and by his relative mildness in dealing with Wilson.

From 1912 until March 31, 1916, the two men did not
even meet. Roosevelt set the pattern by omitting all mention of Root from his autobiography, published in 1913,
and by refusing to invite the Roots to his daughter's wed-
ding that same year. The Bacon luncheon in 1916 produced
negligible results. Rumors persisted that Root had been
induced to cut out of his Carnegie Hall speech in February
all laudatory references to the colonel, while both before
and during the Republican Convention of that year Roosevelt would not even consider Root as a compromise candidate.

During 1917 the old associates often spoke from the
same platform and for the same cause, but the first extant
letter to pass between them after 1912 is dated March 4,
1918. A few other bits of correspondence, outwardly
cordial, were exchanged that year; but Root did not join —
whether he was invited to is not clear — Roosevelt and
Taft in their public rejoinder to Wilson's ill-fated October
appeal for a democratic Congress. On November 26, 1918,
at Roosevelt's request, Root and Henry White conferred
with the ailing colonel in the hospital regarding the peace
terms. That was, apparently, their last meeting. Six weeks
later the Rough Rider reached the end of the trail.

If Roosevelt had lived, he and Root might have worked
harmoniously during the initial stages of the treaty fight,
but it is doubtful whether that unity could have been
maintained to the end. On the other hand, Root would
probably have backed Roosevelt for the nomination in
1920; if elected, Roosevelt would have doubtless made
Root Secretary of State.

The friendship with Taft began later and lasted longer.
It was subjected to many stresses and strains, but a com-

plete break never occurred. The pair first met around 1890 while arguing a case before the Supreme Court. Root must have approved, if he did not suggest, the selection of Taft in 1900 to head the Second Philippine Commission. Intimacy dated from January 1902, when the Roots rescued an enfeebled governor general, while in Washington to testify on conditions in the islands, from a hotel existence. Although Taft was twelve years Root's junior and had been his subordinate in the Philippines and his sucessor in the War Department, Root in 1908 concurred in Roosevelt's judgment that Taft was the most available candidate. Root entered the Senate in 1909 determined to aid his friend in every way.

It was Root's staunch support in the harrowing days of 1912 that forged in Taft a debt of gratitude that no subsequent disagreement or disappointment could wipe out. He appreciated only too well the conflict of loyalties that wracked Root at that time, and he understood only too clearly that Athos did not love Porthos less but D'Artagnan more. Hence he was ready to forgive Root's refusal to campaign actively against Roosevelt and to overlook, as Secretary of State Knox was not, Root's lukewarm backing of the arbitration treaties of 1911 and his outright opposition to the Panama Tolls Act of 1912.

The nadir of the Root-Taft friendship was reached between 1915 and 1920. The major irritant was Root's unwillingness to endorse the League to Enforce Peace. Another was the tight hold he maintained on the purse strings of the Carnegie Corporation and the Carnegie Endowment for International Peace, on the governing boards of which Root served. In his quest for grants to various charitable and educational institutions, Taft found Root, so he complained, "more difficult to deal with than millionaires themselves." He also regarded Root as too partisan in his references to Wilson; and while he publicly stated that Root was the ablest man the Republicans could nominate in 1916, he privately favored Hughes as the wiser choice. Most important of all, Taft deplored Root's stand on the Covenant — his refusal to speak at the Metropolitan Opera House on March 4, 1919, his close cooperation with Lodge, and his partial reversal on Article X.

On his side, Root considered Taft hopelessly idealistic about the League to Enforce Peace and utterly unrealistic at the start of the treaty fight. He tried, however, to avoid argument by ignoring the difference between them and by resorting to banter. On December 1, 1915, for example, after Taft had invited him to deliver the Storrs Lectures at the Yale Law School, where he was teaching, the New Yorker replied: "For a time I considered whether I would not retaliate for your . . . unprovoked attack upon me . . . by accepting and delivering a series . . . so brilliant, profound and epoch-making that they would conclude to discharge you from your position and in lieu of listening to you any further read my lectures aloud every succeeding year."

Early in 1920, the two men drew closer together again. As Lodge swung over to the irreconcilables and as Wilson remained intransigent, Root and Taft found themselves agreeing that the only way out of the impasse was to ratify the treaty with the November reservations or something like them. Both were disappointed by the second defeat in March; both wanted a forthright stand in the Republican platform. It was at Taft's urging — though Lowell prompted Taft — that Root in May 1920 tried vainly to commit Lodge to such a policy. Taft was displeased with the Chicago compromise plank; but by September he agreed with Root that Harding's victory was inevitable and that, under the circumstances, it would be wise to bind him to some pro-League position. Taft approved of the statement of the thirty-one Republicans and would have signed it if he had been accessible. After the election, he was the loudest advocate of putting Root back in the State Department. Throughout the 1920's the two elder states-men corresponded and visited together as the Athos and Porthos of old.

Like Roosevelt before 1909, Taft never tired of asserting that Root was the ablest statesman he had ever known. In a final estimate of January 10, 1926, to his daughter, Taft wrote: "He is certainly one of the strongest men intellec-tually whom I ever met, and he has a judicial cast of mind and power of analysis that are much like Lincoln's. . . . He has not the qualities of leadership that Roosevelt had . . . but his judgment . . . was much more trust-worthy . . . He was a most admirable complement to Roosevelt . . . and it was only after Roosevelt cut himself loose from Root's influence that he made the really great mistakes of his life."

Root's valedictory was rendered more directly. Writing on February 3, 1930, nine days after Taft's resignation as Chief Justice, he said: "It is a little consolation dear boy to believe that you may now find years of restful and happy memories amid universal honor and affection after your amazing career of usefulness and fame. . . . Much water has gone under the mill since that day nearly forty years ago when we argued the Conqueror case in the Supreme Court. During all that time my admiration and deep affec-tion for you dear Porthos have continually increased." Four weeks later Athos became the last of the musketeers.

The least known and perhaps the least admired of Root's friendships was with Henry Cabot Lodge. This is not the place to criticize the caricature that some historians and most journalists have made of the real Lodge. He had his faults, many of them; but it would be unfair to Root and wholly inaccurate to regard the Massachusetts

Senator as the evil genius of Roosevelt, the betrayer of Hay, the slanderer of Taft, and the chief architect of the separate peace. What is pertinent is the reasons for the close ties that existed between Root and Lodge for thirty years after they first met about 1892.

Root and Lodge had common friends, held common beliefs, and shared common dislikes. Temperamentally they were much the same. In domestic politics they were both unabashed conservatives, with an unshakable faith in the efficiency of American business enterprise, in the wisdom of judicial supremacy, and in the indispensability of Republican rule. In foreign policy they accepted the new role of the United States as a global power. They agreed that the old isolationism was dead, that this country had a stake in world peace; but they were reluctant to yield an iota of national sovereignty and determined to make no promises that could not be redeemed in time of crisis. One other bond was Root's affection and admiration for Mrs. Lodge, a lady of immense charm, whose untimely death in September 1915 was an incalculable loss to her husband.

From their friendship Lodge probably derived the greater benefit. While in the cabinet, Root received the Senator's support on such matters as legislation for the Philippines, reform of the consular service, reorganization of the army, and the Algeciras Treaty. In May 1902, Lodge loyally defended on the Senate floor the Secretary of War, who was then being berated by Democrats and anti-imperialists for allegedly suppressing reports of atrocities during the Filipino Insurrection. When Root entered the upper house in 1909, the two men stood together in opposing the direct election of Senators, the Panama Tolls Act, the Ship Purchase bill, Wilson's Mexican policy in 1914, and the New Freedom in general. But it was after Root had retired from office and especially during the treaty fight that Lodge repeatedly called for help. The constancy

with which Root responded to those appeals has been detailed in an earlier chapter. Not once between March 1919
and March 1920 did he fail to do what Lodge requested,
and at least twice he went out of his way to laud the course
the Massachusetts Senator was pursuing.

On several occasions in these later years Lodge failed to
repay those acts of friendship. He did not back Root in
1916, although the New Yorker represented his brand of
Republicanism. He spurned Root's suggestions for some
compromise after the first Senate vote in November 1919.
He turned a deaf ear to Root's plea in May 1920 that the
party platform endorse the Versailles Treaty with suitable
reservations. During the ensuing Presidential campaign
he shared the fears of the irreconcilables that Root's labors
at The Hague were ill-timed, if not ill-advised; after the
triumph in November he twice wrote Harding to oppose
Root as Secretary of State.

The significance of these divergences is not that they
existed, but that Root accepted them without complaint.
He always credited Lodge with complete sincerity of purpose and never resented any difference of opinion.

At the end of Lodge's life, however, Root at last suffered
serious misgivings. After coming to the Senator's aid in the
debate over the Colombian Treaty in 1921 and during his
bid for re-election in 1922, he was annoyed by Lodge's
stubborn refusal to back the Harding-Hughes plan in 1923
for joining the World Court. His wrath neared the boiling
point a year later after Lodge's part in abrogating the gentlemen's agreement with Japan. When Root talked to
Stimson about this on October 28, 1924, a fortnight before
the Senator's death, "his eyes filled with tears and he said
that nothing but lifelong affection for Lodge prevented
him from actual denunciation of his conduct." Root felt
bitterly that his friend should go back on a long career of
honorable dealing with Japan and affront her needlessly.

But he was charitable enough to concede that the death of his wife and of Roosevelt had deprived Lodge of his two main stabilizing influences; soon thereafter he assured Bishop William Lawrence that "Cabot was a man of absolute fidelity. I know no one whose word I would accept with greater confidence."

One other type of friendship remains to be mentioned. That is the bond Root forged with younger men. The admiration that Hay, Lodge, Taft, and Roosevelt repeatedly expressed for Root's brains and acumen was echoed in more worshipful form by persons like Henry L. Stimson, Robert Bacon, Chandler P. Anderson, and James B. Scott. To such a group, Root was the fount of all wisdom, and with fanatical loyalty they tried to spur him on to greater effort and to elevate him to higher office. The most influential and interesting of these juniors was Stimson, whose career and temperament, and even the cut of his hair, resembled Root's. Stimson got his start in Root's law firm, followed him as United States attorney, Secretary of War, and Secretary of State, served with him in the New York Constitutional Convention of 1915, and jointly participated in various preparedness and patriotic organizations during the World War. Stimson looked upon Root as almost a second father; for over a quarter of a century the two men conferred together on every major issue, domestic and foreign, as well as on many personal problems.

With one prominent statesman of the times, Root was never on truly friendly terms. He had known Woodrow Wilson prior to March 1913, but neither before nor after that date could he arouse any enthusiasm or admiration for the man. It was not that Wilson was a Democrat — Root had loved Whitney and had respected Grover Cleveland — but rather that his political principles and his manner of dealing with people rubbed Root the wrong way. The steady deterioration in their personal relations while Root was in the Senate and their outright antagonism afterward have already been set forth. The President after 1915 grew increasingly sensitive to Root's criticism, while the former secretary became convinced that the chief executive was bungling the conduct of the war and the negotiation of the peace. If co-operation had been possible, it is likely that a treaty with acceptable reservations would have passed; and historians with a Wilsonian philosophy have blamed Root for subordinating his better instincts to party unity, personal hatred, and stubborn pride.

That Root's approach to the peace settlement was colored by a conviction that he could have done a better job, as well as by partisan considerations, has been conceded; but it should be remembered that Wilson yielded to the same emotions. The President's reasons for not making Root a commissioner were unworthy of a national leader, and his bitterness was fully disclosed in July 1920. At that time the League of Nations wanted three jurists of international repute to advise the Council on the Aaland Islands dispute, and Root's name was suggested. Both the Secretary of State and the ambassador in England approved, especially since Root was then at The Hague helping to draft the World Court statute. Although the interests of the United States were in no way concerned, Wilson savagely rejected the proposal, saying, "I have absolutely no faith in Mr. Elihu Root and feel sure that he would do something to prove his falseness if we delegated him to act."

There is no evidence that either man ever came, before his death, to think better of the other.

3. *The Root Contribution*

In any summary appraisal of Root's contribution to his times, the years before 1899 are of minor importance. Whatever view one may take of his legal practice and however much his social philosophy and political outlook were shaped by it, Root the lawyer did not vitally influence the nation's history or the American conservative tradition.

It was after entering McKinley's cabinet that Root devised policies, enunciated principles, and provided an example of efficient administration that left their mark on his and later generations. Five contributions stand out. The first was the colonial system established between 1900 and 1902. Confronted with new and unprecedented imperial problems, Root fashioned machinery that insured for politically backward peoples a responsible, honest, and disinterested rule, one that compared favorably with that of more experienced empires. It represented at the time a reasonable compromise between the national interest of the United States and the particular aspirations of the natives. It was designed to fit the needs of the hour; inevitably it became obsolete as the dependencies readied themselves for autonomy or even freedom itself and as enthusiasm at home for overseas possessions died away.

A second contribution was an intelligent and forward-looking administration of the army. The creation of the General Staff, the establishment of the War College, the revision of the militia system, and the suppression with limited manpower of the Filipino Insurrection constitute a record unmatched by any previous peacetime Secretary of War. Less tangible, but even more important, was Root's understanding of the military mind, his concept of the role the army should play in a democracy, and his insistence upon the principle of civilian supremacy. Few secretaries have been more admired and loved by the professional soldier.

In his anticipation of the Good Neighbor policy, Root made a third contribution to his times. Perhaps "attitude" rather than "policy" is a more correct word; for Root did not envisage a comprehensive system of treaties involving consultation, nonintervention, and reciprocal assistance. Eager to bury the recriminations and fears of the past and to inspire friendship and confidence for the future, he injected a new spirit, a new tolerance in dealing with Latin America.

A fourth and more general contribution was a realistic approach to diplomacy, an approach that embraced a proper regard for means as well as ends, an acute understanding of what was attainable at the hour, and a healthy respect for the constitutional framework within which statesmen must operate. Root fully appreciated after 1899 that nineteenth-century isolationism was dead and that the United States, for better or for worse, had become a world power. He freely acknowledged that twentieth-century America had a stake in and a responsibility for the maintenance of peace in Europe and in Asia. He was even ready to conclude permanent defensive alliances with a few major powers, such as France and England. But it did not follow, in his opinion, that the times were ripe or the people prepared for an ambitious international organization that would employ armed strength to enforce its decisions and to defend the territorial integrity or political independence of every member. Root preferred to experiment with machinery more in line with the American tradition. He was an internationalist, but not a Wilsonian; for Wilsonism, in his mind, represented too sharp a break with the past.

A final contribution to his times was Root's outspoken defense of conservatism. In an age eager for constitutional change, he opposed almost every alteration of the basic charter; to the demand that government be made more directly responsible to the people, he countered with a brief for the superiority of representative institutions. In the face of a vast accretion of Federal power, he urged the states to reassert their regulatory authority in social legislation; against every inroad on the rights of private property he issued sterner and sterner protests. At a time when many citizens were carried away by the New Nationalism, the New Freedom, and the New Deal, he stressed the older ways and warned that, in their zeal for a broader concept of democracy, Americans must not ignore the need for efficient administration and the values of the conservative tradition. His was a useful, though not always constructive, voice of caution in an era of change.

Root was not an original or systematic political thinker. He did not, as he once said of Theodore Roosevelt, originate great truths, but strove rather to keep the tested and tried before the eyes of his countrymen. His reputation as a conservative spokesman rests partly on his character, partly on the relative inarticulateness of his group, and partly on his forthright writings and speeches. With all their shortcomings, Root's ideas provide the most useful reply to the progressive challenge.

4. Root's Place in History

It is not enough for the biographer to describe Root's public career and to isolate his most enduring contributions to foreign policy, the administration of government, and the defense of conservatism. He has still to indicate how Root is regarded today and what is likely to be his reputation tomorrow. Time has a way of playing strange and cruel tricks on famous men, and he who looms large in the eyes of one generation may be forgotten by another.

In appearing before the bar of history, Root has two advantages. One is the biography by Philip C. Jessup, a full-length portrait, drawn with sympathy and understanding but free from idolatry. To Root was granted the greatest boon any statesman could ask: the opportunity to converse with his biographer, to pass judgment upon his contemporaries, and to explain his own actions. Because both author and subject strove to be objective and fair, Root's place in history will be partly determined by that work.

The second asset in his battle with the verdict of time is that Root outlived most of the bitter controversies of his day and died universally respected. Except for Woodrow Wilson and William Randolph Hearst, there are few of his prominent contemporaries whose reputations are likely to require an assault upon his. The biographers of McKinley, Hay, Roosevelt, Taft, and Lodge, for example, can all write sympathetically of Root without injury or prejudice to their own man.

To his conflict with oblivion, however, Root brings certain liabilities which, in the long run, may prove fatal. First, there is the nature of his personality. He was not an inspiring speaker, a popular writer, or an uninhibited correspondent. In contrast to Wilson and the two Roosevelts, Root's record on paper can never fully convey his strength, character, and insight. There is a danger that he may suffer the lot of McKinley, whose magnetic charm and ability to bend people to his will have never been recaptured or appreciated by the historian.

Root is exposed to a similar peril by the nature of his philosophy. When he died, his brand of conservatism was at a discount. It is possible, of course, that a coming gen-

eration may look with more favor upon his simple affirma-
tion of nineteenth-century beliefs; but if Root could not
fire the imagination of his contemporaries, it is unlikely he
will move men's minds and hearts in the future. As Elting
E. Morison has perceptively remarked in his introduction
to the fifth volume of *The Letters of Theodore Roosevelt*,
the conservative always labors under a handicap in seeking
the acclaim of posterity.

> The liberal position is easily transportable . . . into the
> future. The great liberal generalizations, placed as they can be
> and often are in statements of compelling beauty, may be
> handed down from generation to generation . . . The con-
> servative position is not so easily transportable. The concentra-
> tion on method, the concern with process . . . rooted as they
> are in the contemporary situation, tend to lose their meaning
> with the passage of time.

Finally, Root's fame is endangered by the nature of his
achievement. His outstanding successes were scored as an
administrator, as a conciliator, as a deviser of workable
solutions to concrete problems. All these tasks were rooted
deep in contemporary situations. Whether he realized it
or not, his chief aim as a public official was to make democracy function in an age of corporate leviathans and to make
democracy survive in a world of competing power. Yet history has been kinder to the rebel, the prophet, the general,
and the martyr, to those who build for the future and draft
blueprints for the age that is waiting before, than to those
who insure an orderly administration of affairs in their own
day.

What, then, can be said of the value placed today on the
Root contribution and of the estimate likely to be made tomorrow?

For his accomplishment in organizing and supervising
an efficient colonial system, Root receives some credit but

little glory. Americans no longer take pride in the imperialistic adventure, and the leaders will never become folk heroes. The enthusiasms of 1898 are not likely to recur.

For his reforms of the army, on the other hand, Root has been lavishly praised, and those tributes will not diminish as the years pass. To be sure, some of the encomiums have been uncritical; for Root laid only the foundation of the complex defense establishment of the present day. But his doctrine of civilian supremacy and the concept of command relationships are as sound now as in 1903; and his sympathetic understanding of the problems of a professional soldier in a democracy initiated a tradition which has been dutifully carried on by men like Henry L. Stimson, Lindley M. Garrison, Robert P. Patterson, and Robert A. Lovett.

The new spirit that Root injected into dealings with Latin America has earned him among historians a place with Clay, Blaine, and Hull as the great protagonists of hemispheric solidarity. There has been some dissent from that view because Root never repudiated the Roosevelt Corollary. A few critics have accused him of being motivated primarily by a desire to sell more goods to southern neighbors.

In the realm of international co-operation, Root's fame has suffered with the passing of the years. The ardent Wilsonians have never forgiven his refusal to join the League to Enforce Peace, his insistence upon reservations to the Versailles Treaty, his part in the equivocal Republican platform of 1920, and his signing the statement of the thirty-one. More important is the fact that the Wilsonian principle inherent in Article X has tended to prevail over the Rootian emphasis upon arbitration, a world court, and the codification of international law. At San Francisco in 1945, the diplomats, intent on drafting an acceptable charter, shrank from the sweeping commitments of the Covenant; but the logic of events in June 1950 led to the very decision that Root, thirty years earlier, would not pledge in advance.

Although the whirligig of time may have vindicated Wilson's cherished Article X, it does not follow that Root in 1920 was unsound in his analysis of what the traffic would then bear. The course of American foreign policy after 1921, whether wise or unwise, demonstrated conclusively that Root, rather than Wilson, saw more clearly that the Covenant broke too sharply with tradition to be then acceptable to the people. Faced with an unhappy dilemma, Root steered some Republicans and many of his countrymen on to a middle road, one that answered some needs of the hour, and tried to maintain a concern for world peace in the party of Roosevelt and Taft. During the late 1930's, internationalist Republicans were at a premium; but thanks to Stimson, Frank Knox, and a few others, the Root tradition was kept alive and transmitted to postwar leaders like Arthur H. Vandenberg, Thomas E. Dewey, and Henry Cabot Lodge, Jr.

As a defender of the conservative tradition, Root seems strangely outmoded. Most of the innovations he combated have become part of the nation's life. Inevitably, the conservative of yesterday becomes the reactionary of today, just as the liberal of today becomes the conservative of tomorrow. In domestic affairs, Root will always be regarded by some as "the attorney for capitalism" in late nineteenth-century America, a candid, shrewd lawyer-politician with "a full grown class conscious point of view." Root never matched the creative achievements of Hamilton and Marshall and will, therefore, always rank below them on the roster of American conservatives. But more than anyone of his philosophy in the first quarter of the twentieth century, he did sense the inherent stresses and strains in the modern industrial state, and he did recognize that to keep the powerful machine functioning properly judicious concessions were necessary, if only to avoid radical reform. "Growth," he liked to say, "is the law of life and the perennial problem is how to hold fast to what is good and essential and at the same time substitute new growth for dead matter."

As the unending battle between liberalism and conservatism surges into the future, the cause of the latter could benefit from a little more daring, imagination, and faith in the people than Root was able to contribute; but it can never do without his integrity and fair-mindedness, his intelligence and good humor, his intuitive judgment and mastery of the facts, his respect for efficient administration and insistence upon balancing power with responsibility.

A Note on the Sources

THE STANDARD LIFE, in fact the only one, is Philip C. Jessup, *Elihu Root* (2 vols., 1938). As the official biographer, Professor Jessup enjoyed unusual advantages. A graduate of Hamilton College, an assistant to Root at the Conference of Jurists on the Permanent Court of International Justice in 1929, an eminent authority on international law with experience in practical diplomacy, he was able to draft much of the book during Root's lifetime. He could, therefore, question his subject and obtain oral and written statements on controversial or doubtful points. Yet he was left remarkably free to reach his own conclusions and interpretations, for Root never asked to see what had been written. Professor Jessup had access not only to the Root Papers in the Library of Congress and personal letters still in family hands but also to the manuscript collections of a wide array of Root's contemporaries, some of whom read and criticized pertinent chapters. Painstaking in research, fair in judgment, lavish in detail, fully documented and with copious quotations from letters and speeches, the eleven hundred pages of the Jessup volumes represent a major achievement in recent American biography. The debt of the present writer to them is very great indeed, even though his appraisal of Elihu Root is not the same.

This book is designed to acquaint the general reader with the significance of Root's public service and its meaning for today. It is hoped that it may, incidentally, provide the professional scholar with an interpretation and evaluation that differ from the Jessup portrait in several important respects. No attempt has been made to cover all phases of Root's long and varied career. The treatment is selective rather than comprehensive; and although it follows a chronological pattern, the amount of space allotted to each topic does not correspond, even roughly, to the number of years in Root's life that it occupied.

As an outgrowth of a multivolume study of the United States as a world power, this biography is based upon an independent examination of the many manuscript and printed sources used by Professor Jessup and upon a perusal of certain personal papers and specialized works that were not available when he wrote. These fresh materials were most helpful for chapters four, five, six, and eight.

The essential manuscripts were, of course, the Root Papers. Those in the Library of Congress cover, for the most part, the years from 1899 to 1937, and they are fullest for the period from July 1899 to March 1915. They are fragmentary for much of the World War, disappointing for the peacemaking, and inadequate for the Washington Conference. Nor do they contain the requisite data for a description or an analysis of Root's law practice. For certain aspects of Root's public activity while out of office, his scrapbooks in the New York Public Library are useful.

Among the private papers utilized by Professor Jessup, the following were reinvestigated for this biography (all are in the Library of Congress unless otherwise indicated): Chandler P. Anderson, Andrew Carnegie, Joseph H. Choate, Henry C. Corbin, John W. Foster, John Hay, Philander C. Knox, Henry Cabot Lodge (Massachusetts Historical Society), William McKinley, John T. Morgan, Theodore Roosevelt, John C. Spooner, Henry L. Stimson (Yale University), and William Howard Taft. It is believed that because they have been better arranged or made more accessible since 1938, the Taft, Lodge, and Stimson Papers have yielded new information, especially concerning Root's part during the battle over the Treaty of Versailles.

Among the manuscript collections not available in 1938,

the following were consulted: Albert J. Beveridge, Tasker H. Bliss, William E. Borah, Charles G. Dawes (Northwestern University), George Dewey, Francis V. Greene (New York Public Library), Frederick W. Holls (Columbia University), Charles E. Hughes, Robert Lansing, A. Lawrence Lowell (Harvard University), David H. Miller, William H. Moody, Richard Olney, Gifford Pinchot, Charles E. Russell, Hugh L. Scott, Albert Shaw (New York Public Library), Oscar S. Straus, Henry White, William Allen White, William C. Whitney, and Woodrow Wilson.

Eight volumes of Root's writings and addresses, covering the period through 1923, were edited by Robert Bacon and James B. Scott, and published between 1916 and 1925. They contain his main speeches and articles, extracts from the War Department reports and State Department instructions, and the whole of his Dodge Lectures at Yale in 1907 (*The Citizen's Part in Government*) and of his Stafford Little Lectures at Princeton in 1913 (*Experiments in Government and the Essentials of the Constitution*). These are entitled *Addresses on Government and Citizenship* (1916), *Addresses on International Subjects* (1916), *Latin America and the United States* (1917), *Men and Policies* (1925), *Miscellaneous Addresses* (1917), *North Atlantic Coast Fisheries Arbitration at The Hague* (1917), *The Military and Colonial Policy of the United States* (1916), and *The United States and the War, The Mission to Russia, Political Addresses* (1918). There is a valuable chronological list of Root's principal public speeches and papers in Jessup, II, 521–552. Other primary materials are to be found in the printed and unprinted records of the War and State Departments, in the *Congressional Record* and various reports and hearings of the Senate committees, in pamphlets, and in contemporary newspapers and magazines.

There is no good study of the "corporation lawyer" and his contribution to American development after 1865. The classic description of acquisitive America is in Charles A. and Mary R. Beard, *The Rise of American Civilization* (2 vols., 1927).

On the background of Root's labors as Secretary of War, see Julius W. Pratt, *America's Colonial Experiment* (1950);

Oliver L. Spaulding, *The United States Army in War and Peace* (1937); Otto L. Nelson, *National Security and the General Staff* (1946); and William T. Sexton, *Soldiers in the Sun: an Adventure in Imperialism* (1939). The literature on the Philippines is voluminous, but it is either polemical in nature or insufficiently grounded on the vast amount of manuscript material now available.

A general survey of Root's tenure in the State Department is given in James B. Scott, "Elihu Root," *American Secretaries of State and Their Diplomacy* (S. F. Bemis, ed., 10 vols., 1927–1929), IX, 193–282. The role of the United States in world affairs between 1905 and 1909 remains to be written. Jessup has dealt more fully than any monograph with Root's efforts in Latin America and Canada. Thomas A. Bailey's *Theodore Roosevelt and the Japanese-American Crises* (1934) is a judicious analysis.

The best account of the split in the Republican party after 1909 is in George E. Mowry, *Theodore Roosevelt and the Progressive Movement* (1946). Alpheus T. Mason's *Bureaucracy Convicts Itself* (1941) is fullest on the Ballinger-Pinchot controversy. Its hostility toward Root and its lavish praise of Brandeis might have been modified if its author could have examined certain personal papers now available. Arthur S. Link's *Woodrow Wilson and the Progressive Era* (1954) is a superb account of both domestic and foreign affairs from 1910 to April 1917.

Writings on America's road to war are almost endless, but none describes adequately the position of men like Root. Charles C. Tansill, *America Goes to War* (1938), based upon extensive research for its day, is predicated on the assumption that American participation was a ghastly mistake. For an appraisal of this literature, see Richard W. Leopold, "The Problem of American Intervention, 1917: an Historical Retrospect," *World Politics*, II (April 1950), 405–425.

On the background and course of the peacemaking, see three able works: Ruhl J. Bartlett's *The League to Enforce Peace* (1944), which is very critical of Root, and Thomas A. Bailey's readable *Woodrow Wilson and the Lost Peace* (1944) and *Woodrow Wilson and the Great Betrayal* (1945).

There is no balanced, up-to-date account of American diplomacy from 1921 to 1937. Despite its ardent Wilsonism, Denna F. Fleming's *The United States and World Organization, 1920–1933* (1938) is still useful, but much printed diplomatic correspondence and many collections of personal papers have become available since it was published. There is an excellent narrative of the Washington Conference in Harold and Margaret Sprout, *Toward a New Order of Sea Power* (1940).

Among the biographies of Root's contemporaries, Mark C. Hirsch, *William C. Whitney: Modern Warwick* (1948) rounds out the picture of the consolidation of Manhattan's street railways. Tyler Dennett, *John Hay: from Poetry to Politics* (1933) is a keen appraisal of men and events, marred only by its animus toward Lodge. Henry F. Pringle, *Theodore Roosevelt* (1931) is provocative and amusing but does something less than justice to its subject. A more balanced portrait of the twenty-sixth President emerges from *The Letters of Theodore Roosevelt* (Elting E. Morison, ed., 8 vols., 1951–1954). Pringle's *Life and Times of William Howard Taft* (2 vols., 1939) is a maturer book, but it is thin on the battle over the peace treaty. *Henry Cabot Lodge: a Biography* (1953) by John A. Garraty makes full use of the rich Lodge Papers. Merlo J. Pusey, *Charles Evans Hughes* (2 vols., 1951) is helpful in certain places; but, in general, it lacks depth and a critical spirit. Henry L. Stimson and McGeorge Bundy, *On Active Service in Peace and War* (1948) is a unique autobiography that aids enormously in understanding Root and his major disciple.

Acknowledgments

THE AUTHOR is indebted to the Committee on Research Funds of the Graduate School of Northwestern University for its support of this and allied projects and to Dean Simeon E. Leland, of the College of Liberal Arts, for providing a leave of absence in which to complete the writing. He is also under deep obligation to the following friends, scholars all, who have criticized and improved thereby the manuscript: Oscar Handlin of Harvard University and editor of The Library of American Biography, Edward Mead Earle of The Institute for Advanced Study, Elting E. Morison and John M. Blum of the Massachusetts Institute of Technology, McGeorge Bundy of Harvard University, and his invaluable colleagues, Ray A. Billington and Arthur S. Link of Northwestern University. The last has been particularly generous in discussing the work at every stage and in sharing his unrivaled knowledge of the Wilson period. It does not follow that all of the foregoing agree with the appraisal of Root found in these pages. The author wishes to thank also Margaret D. Link, who took time from more pressing duties to aid with the galleys, and Ronald W. Dempelein, Northwestern University, class of 1954, who examined the manuscript in the capacity of that elusive individual, the general reader. Mrs. Joyce Tyler of Little, Brown and Company was most helpful and patient in preparing the manuscript for publication.

RICHARD W. LEOPOLD

Evanston, Illinois
September 1953

INDEX

Index

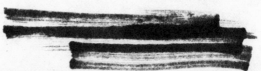